Pearson's Canal Companion

Four Counties Ring

affectionately dedicated to the memory of John Stothert of Audlem

Published by Wayzgoose
Tatenhill Common
Staffordshire DE13 9RS
email: enquiries@jmpearson.co.uk
www.jmpearson.co.uk

WAYZGOOSE

Post-industrial Potteries ...

... the Trent & Mersey at Etruria

A MBLING along the Caldon Canal one warm April afternoon, a mood of benediction fell upon me. Replete with two of Emma Bridgewater's estimable cheese and bacon oatcakes (she dabbles in crockery to equally good effect), and keenly anticipating a sojourn in Milton's invariably well-stocked second-hand bookshop, I found myself echoing Dean Friedman's tuneful sentiments from the year when I began to earn my living on the inland waterways, 'thanking my lucky stars' that this was work, if not how millions know it. Not that it has all been Roses & Castles: chronic impecunity (no one professionally employed in or around the inland waterways ever made much money); a time-consuming and cyclically blinkered vision that effectively prevented me from spreading my literary wings (though whether or not I would have been able to fly is open to conjecture); and now, coming home to roost after years of towpath pounding and running between lock chambers, a pair of recalcitrantly aching feet, seemingly determined to curtail my researches, the canal explorer's equivalent of Postman's Foot: Towpath Toes perhaps. And me, the Tintin of inland waterway guidebook compilation, how did this come to pass?

But it was too invigorating a day to throw in the towel, and it was too good to be back in The Potteries - one of those irrevocably damaged parts of England with which I feel a natural affinity - to pander to the demands of an ageing body. Overtaking a family party on the towpath, the grandmother had pulled a dawdling toddler aside with a pure North Staffordshire imprecation to 'mind the master'. A man leaning avuncularly over a garden wall had asked if I could identify a fish floating on the surface: 'Chubb, Dace?' I ventured, no expert when it came to coarse varieties, my father having been a dry fly man, but he nodded his head sagaciously, as between two men of the piscatorial world. And in Abacas Bookshop the talk had turned to Arnold Bennett and the current dearth of radio, television or film adaptations of his work. In his nineteen-twenties

Lock-wheeling

pomp, Bennett was better known throughout the bibliophilic western world than Wedgwood. Now, inexplicably, he sells less books on Amazon than me. So much for *Ars longa, vita brevis*.

A few days later I was fortunate enough to be given a guided tour of Middleport Pottery, the one which aficionados are pretty certain Bennett used as a model for Henry Mynors' Providence Works in *Anna of the Five Towns*. Here, it seemed to me, past, present and future were being profitably melded together in such a manner as to defy those who would have it that time-honoured working practices have no part to play in the modern world. Emerging from the subfusc interior of the bottle kiln - one part of the process which the Clean Air Act *has* called time on - I glanced through a window and saw two men manhandling biscuit-ware between departments, a timeless cameo straight from the image of Victor Skellern's which adorned the Penguin Modern Classics 1970s edition of the novel. Truly, in The Potteries, time is chronologically untrustworthy. That very evening, the Arnold Bennett Society were giving a showing of the 1952 film of *The Card*, starring a youthful Alec Guinness as Denry Machin, and I was sorry to be missing it, because it would have put the seal on my born again baptism in the redeeming waters of what the boatmen of the past vernacularly referred to as the 'North Staffs Cut'.

Outside, boats were chugging by. Not, alas, bearing coal or china clay, nor departing with consignments of Burleigh Ware, but at least they were keeping the Trent & Mersey on a life support machine. Besides, I couldn't quibble, for this post-industrial leisure revival has kept the wolf from my door for the best part of forty years, during the course of which I have inadvertently acquired something of a cult status along the undredged backwaters of inland waterway journalism. So where does that leave me and my ailing feet? Perhaps, as Mr. Friedman continued, 'I am not as smart as I like to think I am'. Not a 'master', then, let alone a big fish in a small pond. More like a pike in a puddle.

Caldon Canal near Milton

Aston Lock

T. & S. ELEMENTS LTD
BIRMINGHAM & OLDBURY

Trent & Mersey Canal

5

THE junction between the Trent & Mersey and Bridgewater canals lies, somewhat mysteriously, a few yards inside the northern end of Preston Brook Tunnel. Walking the old horse path over the top of the tunnel, you'll come upon milepost 92 in the sequence from Shardlow, the canal's southern terminus. The tunnel isn't wide enough for narrow boats to pass inside, and access is controlled by a timetable - see below. Neither is it exactly straight - being one of the earliest canal tunnels, it seems that Brindley and his staff had yet to perfect the art of digging in a direct line.

At the southern end of the tunnel the Trent & Mersey Company built a stop lock to protect their water supply from being drawn into the Bridgewater Canal. Nearby stands a drydock covered by a valanced canopy which has a distinct railway character. No surprise, for the dock was built by the North Staffordshire Railway - one time owners of the canal - for the maintenance of steam tugs introduced in 1865 to haul boats through the tunnel in the absence of a towpath.

Between Dutton Lock and Bartington Wharf the canal hugs the shoulders of the Weaver Valley, making its way awkwardly across the armpits of a sequence of wooded ravines which must have challenged the canal builder's patience. Challenged modern day maintenance procedures too, for in 2012 a breach at Dutton culminated in the newly formed Canal & River Trust's first public appeal. A lacklustre response forced them to internalise most of the repair costs, and set awkward precedents for funding major repairs in future. Indeed, there was further leakage in 2015. On the skyline beyond Dutton Locks looms an imposing railway viaduct - it carries the West Coast Main Line over the valley. Sixty feet high and totalling twenty arches, it dates from 1837 and is the work of Joseph Locke.

⚠ Southbound boats may enter Preston Brook Tunnel for ten minutes on the half hour; northbound similarly on the hour.

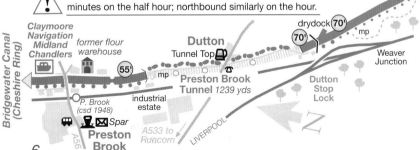

The towpath is mostly wide and flat, though sometimes grassy along this length. Comfortable for walkers, not always so for cyclists.

Summary of Facilities

There is a Spar convenience store within easy reach of the canal at Preston Brook whilst a pub called the TUNNEL TOP (Tel: 01928 718181 - WA4 4JY) stands above Preston Brook Tunnel. It's open from noon daily. BLUEBELL COTTAGE GARDENS can be found just downhill from Bridge 213. Tel: 01928 713718. The garden showcases a range of herbaceous hardy perennials available to purchase from the adjoining organic nursery. Additionally there are bluebell woods and a wildflower meadow to explore. Light refreshments also available. They open 10am-5pm Wed-Sun. WA4 4HP

THE Trent & Mersey revels in its remarkably lovely journey through a rural landscape of rolling farmland interspersed with belts of deciduous woodland, eventually becoming engulfed in the dusky portals of Saltersford and Barnton tunnels. In common with Preston Brook they are just not wide enough to enable narrow boats to pass inside. Barnton is considered short enough for the inherent good manners, invariably associated with boaters, to be discipline enough. Saltersford, on the other hand, has had a timetable introduced in recent years - see below - to minimise unfortunate outbreaks of the sort of brawling traditionally ascribed to working boatmen as opposed to holidaymakers. A broad leafy pool, much favoured by fishermen, separates the two tunnels and the old horse-paths continue to provide walkers with an enjoyably bosky connecting link across the tops.

Of all the so-called "Seven Wonders of the Waterways", Anderton Lift is arguably the most ingenious. Its role is to overcome the fifty feet disparity in level between the Trent & Mersey Canal and Weaver Navigation by lowering or raising boats in two water-filled caissons, each capable of holding a pair of narrowboats. The Lift dates from 1875 and was designed by Edwin Clark. Corrosion of the metal-work brought about its closure in 1983, and it remained embarrassingly out of use for the best part of twenty years until re-opening with £7m of Heritage Lottery funding in 2002, a star visitor attraction in its own right never mind

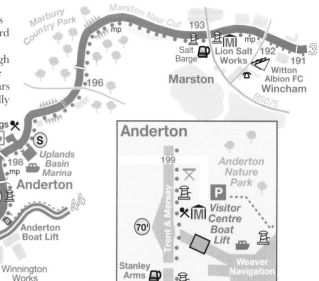

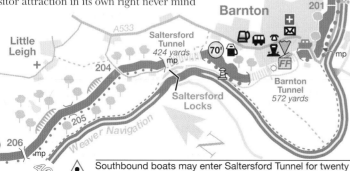

its strategic importance in linking the canal with the Weaver. Holding moorings for boaters intending to use the Lift are located on the Trent & Mersey Canal alongside the Visitor Centre.

East of Anderton the Trent & Mersey winds past Marbury Country Park largely untouched by the outskirts of Northwich, though there are occasional glimpses of the town and its chemical industry nestling down in the valley of the Weaver. Centuries of salt production has destabilised the landscape. In 1958 a new length of canal had to be dug at Marston to by-pass a section troubled by subsidence. Eastwards, the horizon is

continued on page 8

for details of facilities at Barnton and Anderton turn to page 8

⚠ Southbound boats may enter Saltersford Tunnel for twenty minutes on the half hour; northbound similarly on the hour.

7

continued from page 7

dominated by the substantial parish church at Great Budworth.

Lion Salt Works was the last in Britain still producing salt by the process of evaporation in open brine pans. In its heyday the works operated its own small fleet of narrowboats plying between Marston and Anderton where the salt would be transhipped into larger vessels for export through the Mersey ports. Rendered obsolete, it closed in 1986. Thirty years later it has been re-opened as a fascinating visitor centre, telling the story - in a thoroughly entertaining manner - of salt manufacture in this part of the world. Good visitor moorings give no excuse for not stopping!

Between bridges 191 and 192 the canal used to be sandwiched between the stadia of two non-league football teams: Northwich Victoria founded in 1874; and Witton Albion founded in 1887. Sadly, 'The Vics', proud history notwithstanding, no longer play opposite their neighbours. The financial vicissitudes of football - even at a non-league level - saw them evicted from their impressive new stadium beside the Trent & Mersey, resulting in a nomadic existence - currently they play at Flixton.

Barnton Maps 2 & 44

The beauty of the tunnel-framed pool is not necessarily echoed by the village behind it. Nevertheless Barnton provides a useful range of facilities, as depicted on the map, and a 20 minute interval (hourly Sun) bus service (No.4) connects with Northwich.

Anderton Maps 2 & 44

It's nice to linger by The Lift and watch how it takes the breath away. Good visitor moorings provide every excuse to do so, whilst the adjoining country park gives you an opportunity to stretch your legs on the long pound between Preston Brook and Middlewich.

Eating & Drinking

THE MOORINGS - restaurant and coffee shop at Anderton Marina. Tel: 01606 79789. CW9 6AJ
STANLEY ARMS - canalside opposite Anderton Lift. Tel: 01606 75059. Food from noon daily. Greene King ales. Offside customer moorings. CW9 6AG
LIFT CAFETERIA - canalside. Boaters breakfasts available from 9.45am daily at this cafe offering fine views of the Lift. Tel: 01606 786777. CW9 6FW

Things to Do

ANDERTON BOAT LIFT - Tel: 01606 786777. Canalside Visitor Centre celebrating the Lift and local canals in all their historic glory. CW9 6FW

A widebeam trip boat named *Edwin Clark* after the Lift's designer offers trips up or down the Lift. River trips to Northwich and back are also usually available.

ANDERTON NATURE PARK - waymarked trails through reclaimed wasteland where many plants usually confined to coastal environments thrive in the local salty soils. Tel: 01606 77741.

Connections

BUSES - Network Warrington service 46 runs to Northwich bi-hourly Mon-Sat. Tel: 0871 200 2233.
TAXIS - JJ's. Tel: 01606 76262.

Going Down!

Marston Map 2

Former salt mining village still wrought by the lopsided scars of the past.

Eating & Drinking

SALT BARGE - Ollershaw Lane (Bridge 193). Tel: 01606 43064. *Good Beer Guide* listed local offering food 12-2.30pm and 5-9pm Mon-Fri, and from noon at weekends until 9pm Sat, 8.30pm Sun. CW9 6ES
Crusty Cob cafe/sandwich bar 2 mins west of Bridge 192.

Things to Do

LION SALT WORKS - Ollershaw Lane (Bridge 193). Tel: 01606 275040. £10m well-spent on restoring and interpreting an open-pan salt manufactory. Open daily (ex Mon) 10am-5pm. Cafe & shop. CW9 6ES

Wincham Wharf Map 3

Eating & Drinking

NECTARS - Bridge 189. Tel: 01606 333723. Warehouse conversion, live music, over 25s only. CW9 7NT
THE CODFATHER - Manchester Road. Tel: 01606 42342. Excellent fish & chips. CW9 7NE
MR FU's - Manchester Road. Tel: 01606 42246. Chinese buffet. CW9 7NE

Broken Cross Map 3

Canalside at Bridge 184 stands the OLD BROKEN CROSS refurbished in the modern manner - Tel: 01606 40431. CW9 7EB.

PREDOMINANTLY rural in character, the Trent & Mersey Canal makes its way through the peaceful valley of the River Dane, only the suburbs of Broken Cross and the Brunner Mond soda ash works at Lostock contrive to break the bucolic spell. Soda ash has many end uses ranging from foodstuffs to pharmaceuticals. After a period in ICI ownership, the works has reverted to its original name, albeit Indian controlled now. There are plans for a waste-burning power plant to be erected on the site, with fuel being brought in by rail. John Brunner was a Victorian industrialist and politician, his partner, Ludwig Mond, a chemist of German extraction.

A curious feature of this section of the canal are the subsidence-induced flashes bordering the main channel to the south of Bridge 181. They were once filled with the submerged wrecks of abandoned narrowboats, an inland waterway equivalent of Scapa Flow. Many of the boats were brought here and sunk en masse during the Fifties in circumstances almost as controversial in canal terms as the scuttling of the German fleet at Scapa after the First World War. In what was probably a book-keeping exercise, British Waterways rid themselves of surplus narrowboats in a number of watery graves throughout the system. In recent years all the wrecks have been raised and taken off for restoration: one generation's cast-offs become the next's prized possessions.

In the environs of Higher Shurlach, sweet aromas issue forth from Roberts Bakery, established back in 1887. Two million loaves a week are baked here, and in addition to making bread and cakes, the works

The towpath south of Broken Cross was indifferently maintained when we last passed, especially in the vicinity of Whatcroft Hall

is famous for its brass band.

The Northwich to Sandbach line, opened by the London & North Western Railway in 1868, is occasionally used as a diversionary route, though there are aspirations that it might be revived as a commuter link between Northwich and Crewe with a new station opening at Middlewich. Hereabouts the Dane, nearing journey's end at Northwich where it joins the Weaver, has grown sluggish with age, meandering about its level valley in a succession of broad loops, so that at one moment it is hard by the canal, the next away across the fields of milking herds. The soil here is soft and the river carves deep banks shadowed by alder and willow.

Bramble Cuttings

Whatcroft Hall

River Dane

Orchard Marina

Billinge Green Halt (csd 1942)

Northwich – Sandbach (goods only)

A556 to Chester

Broken Cross

lagoons

Higher Shurlach

Roberts Bakery

Old Broken Cross

Rudheath

Co-op

Wincham Wharf

pipes

Brunner Mond

B5082 to Northwich

A559 to Northwich

CHESTER

4 TRENT & MERSEY CANAL Middlewich 5mls/9lks/3hrs*

MIDDLEWICH is one of those arcane places well-known in canal circles but meaningless to most other people. In the old days it was salt which brought so much traffic to Middlewich's canals; the salt boats and, of course, the coal boats without which industry could not function in that pre-electric age. Now, though, it's with pleasure boating that this small town is predominantly concerned, with two hire fleets and a boatyard adding traffic to the often frenetically busy Trent & Mersey Canal.

Five locks punctuate the canal's progress around the eastern edge of the town. The central three - deep and tediously slow to use - are bordered by compounds of stacked pallets and the baleful architecture of small industrial units; all a far cry from the salty scenes of the past, when Seddons and Cerebos were at their zenith and a forest of flaring chimney stacks appeared to support the Middlewich sky.

North of the town, Croxton Aqueduct carries the canal over the River Dane, not far from its confluence with the Wheelock. Originally the aqueduct was built to broad-beam dimensions. Close inspection of the undergrowth reveals some remnants of the old supporting piers. Now, ironically, it is just about the narrowest place between Preston Brook and Middlewich.

Big Lock lives up to its name, recalling the original concept that the canal be capable of handling widebeam craft inland from the Mersey ports as far as Middlewich: that, at least, was the idea, until someone decided to skimp on the tunnels.

No one, alas, appears to be in a hurry to take up the 'Excellent Canalside Development Opportunity' offered by the old Town Wharf by Bridge 172. Strange and sad how some former canal buildings seem so ripe for redevelopment whilst others are stifled and moribund. Yet business seems brisk at the two hire bases. Andersen's fleet brings a taste of the Norwegian fjords to Cheshire, whilst Middlewich Narrowboats' hire base and boatyard, with its old canal managers' house and attractive canopy, strikes a welcome element of dignity. Their drydock was once used by Seddons to maintain their fleet of narrowboats.

Bridge 168 spans what is ostensibly the Shropshire Union Canal's Middlewich Branch, though the first hundred yards were actually built by the Trent & Mersey in a ruse to extract increased tolls. Keep an eye on boat movements here, for Middlewich can suddenly become *Muddlewich* when someone's bow comes shooting out of the Shropshire Union without advance warning. Boaters calling in at King's Lock Chandlery only add to the melee, but cheerfulness should remain the order of the day. Beneath the embankment of a reservoir, the Trent & Mersey heads southwards out of town. British Salt still fly the flag for Middlewich's stock in trade, but the gravy factory which once bordered the canal has sadly bit the dust: not so much 'Ah Bisto' as alas poor Bisto.

*figures refer to Trent & Mersey, Four Counties Ring = 4mls/7lks/3hrs

chemical works
Booth Lane Locks 28ft 9ins
British Salt
waste recycling centre
Rumps Lock 9ft 2ins
4 COUNTIES RING
Middlewich Locks 32ft 7ins
Kings Lock 11ft 3ins
Middlewich (csd 1960)
Wardle Lock 9ft 9ins
Big Lock 5ft 0ins
Town Centre
Middlewich
River Dane
Morrisons
aqueducts
keep to channel!
Croxton Aqueduct
River Wheelock
Stanthorne Lock 11ft 1in
A530 to Nantwich

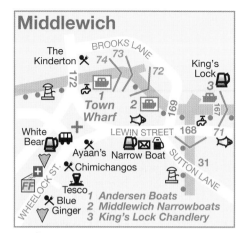

Middlewich

The Kinderton × 74 73 172

BROOKS LANE

72

King's Lock 3

1 *Town Wharf*

2 169

167

White Bear

LEWIN STREET 168 71

Ayaan's × Narrow Boat

× Chimichangos

SUTTON LANE

31

Tesco

× Blue Ginger

1 Andersen Boats
2 Middlewich Narrowboats
3 King's Lock Chandlery

WHEELOCK ST.

FF

Middlewich　　　　　Map 4

A salt making town since the days of the Roman occupation, Middlewich's most interesting building is the parish church of St Michael whose tower remains visibly wounded by missiles unleashed during the Civil War - apparently they're still trying to sort out the insurance. Leaflets are obtainable from the library to guide you around some of the known sites of Roman history. June's 'Folk & Boat' Festival continues to grow in popularity and can be relied upon to wake the town from its customary torpor.

Eating & Drinking

AYAAN'S - High Town. Tel: 01606 836413. Indian restaurant opposite the church. CW10 9AN
BLUE GINGER - Wheelock Street. Tel: 01606 737579. Contemporary Indian open from 5pm. CW10 9AB
CHIMICHANGOS - Wheelock Street. Tel: 01606 836000. Mexico comes to Middlewich. CW10 9AG
THE KINDERTON - adjacent Bridge 172. Tel: 01606 834169. Restaurant with accommodation. CW10 0JE

NARROW BOAT - Lewin Street. Tel: 01606 738087. Welcoming town centre pub. CW10 9AS
WHITE BEAR - Wheelock Street. Tel: 01606 837666. Smartly refurbished pub/restaurant. CW10 9AG
The Big Lock (01606 833489) and King's Lock (Tel: 01606 836894) are canalside pubs.

Shopping

There's a Tesco Express, Tesco supermarket ('off stage' at the back of Wheelock Street) plus Lidl and Morrisons supermarkets at the far end of town. There are two butchers, a pet shop and a pharmacy on Wheelock St.

Connections

BUSES - Arriva service 42 links Middlewich with Congleton and Crewe (for the railway station). Service 37 runs to/from Northwich. Tel: 0871 200 2233.
TAXIS - Sid's. Tel: 01606 833815.

Sandbach　　　　　(Map 5)

Chiefly famous for its ancient Saxon crosses - two lofty and slender stones elaborately carved with biblical scenes including the Nativity and Crucifixion - Sandbach lies about a mile east of the canal at Ettily Heath, though there is easy access to the railway station (from which services run to Crewe, Manchester Airport and Manchester) from Bridge 160 and buses run frequently from Wheelock. The Town Hall - which houses the covered market, open Thur & Sat - is of decidedly Flemish appearance. In transport circles Sandbach was lauded as the home of lorry making. Fodens had their roots in 19th century agricultural machinery and they were at the forefront of the development of steam lorries. Edwin Richard Foden (ERF) broke away from the family business to concentrate on diesel lorries and, seeing how successful he became, the family followed suit. Sadly, though, production is no longer centred on the town, though a well known brass band of that name survives. Much more salubrious than neighbouring Middlewich, some excellent shops and pubs render Sandbach worth a detour. Godfrey C. Williams (Tel:

01270 762817) is a 'specialist grocer and cheese connoisseur' located on the cobbled market square. The Beer Emporium (Tel: 01270 760113) on Welles Street is a micropub and bottled beer outlet, whilst Old Hall (Tel: 01270 758170) on High Street is a classic Brunning & Price pub. There are Aldi and Waitrose supermarkets.

Wheelock　　　　　Map 5

Though by-passed by the A534, Wheelock still endures more than its fair share of traffic - a culture shock after the peace of the canal. Nevertheless, it's a useful pit stop with several opportunities to eat out or acquire fast food.

Eating & Drinking

CHESHIRE CHEESE - Bridge 154. Tel: 01270 760319. Hydes ales, food & beer garden. CW11 3RL
COMMERCIAL HOTEL - adjacent Bridge 154. Tel: 01270 760122. Famous throw-back. Filled baps and Weetwood ales. CW11 3RR
SHAMPAAN - Crewe Road. Tel: 01270 753528. Indian restaurant open from 5pm (4pm Sun). CW11 3RL
Fish & chips (Tel: 01270 768114) and Chinese take-away (Tel: 01270 763169).

Shopping

Convenience store and pet food superstore.

Connections

BUSES - Frequent services Mon-Sat (hourly Sun) to/from Sandbach and Crewe. Tel: 0871 200 2233.

Hassall Green　　　　　Map 5

Downhill, past the kit-built, pink-painted mission church, the old North Staffordshire Railway has been converted into the "Salt Line" bridleway. Generations of pleasure boaters had patronised the post office stores alongside Lock 57, but sadly it closed down in 2012 and the premises have been converted into a private dwelling. Buses run to Sandbach and Alsager.

LOCKS proliferate, and are potentially habit-forming, as the Trent & Mersey ascends from (or descends to) the Cheshire Plain. There are twenty-six chambers to negotiate in only seven miles between Wheelock and Hardings Wood, and "Heartbreak Hill" - as this section has been known to generations of boaters - seems an all too appropriate nickname by the time you have reached the top or bottom; two hundred and fifty feet up or down.

With the exception of the Pierpoint pair, all the locks were 'duplicated' in the 1830s, paddles between adjoining chambers enabling one lock to act as a mini-reservoir to its neighbour. These side paddles were taken out of use when commercial traffic ceased towards the end of the 1960s, but the duplicated locks still ease delays today, though on our most recent cruise we noted a disturbing number 'temporarily' out of use; evidence of the Canal & River Trust's budget being stretched tighter and tighter?

The locks may, or may not, make life hard for the boater, but the canal itself is

illuminated by a succession of small communities with interesting pasts. At Ettily Heath the quadrupled, electrified tracks of the Crewe to Manchester railway cross the canal at the site of a transhipment basin provided to facilitate traffic with the Potteries. Hereabouts the canal, concrete-banked and steel-piled, tends to be deeper than is normal on account of subsidence caused by salt-mining in the past. The River Wheelock rises in the vicinity of Little Moreton Hall and gives its name to a former wharfingering community situated where the Crewe-Sandbach road crossed the canal. Malkin's Bank was home to the families of boatmen engaged in comparatively short-haul traffics connected with the salt and chemical industries. They lived cheek-by-jowl with employees at the huge Brunner-Mond sodium carbonate works which is now buried beneath the greens and fairways of Malkins Bank golf course. New housing has changed the atmosphere somewhat. Between locks 62 and 63, a side bridge carries the towpath over an old arm (now used by a boatbuilder) which once went into the chemical works. Sections of the former North Staffordshire Railway branch line have been adapted for leisure use at Wheelock and Hassall Green.

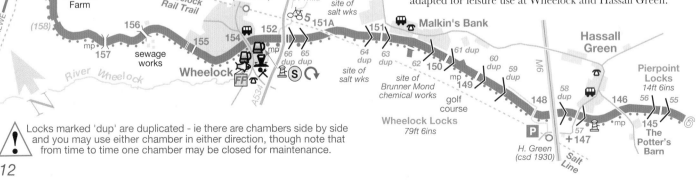

Locks marked 'dup' are duplicated - ie there are chambers side by side and you may use either chamber in either direction, though note that from time to time one chamber may be closed for maintenance.

6 TRENT & MERSEY CANAL Rode Heath & Red Bull 4mls/13lks/3hrs

ONE hardly knows where to begin describing this richly rewarding length of the Trent & Mersey Canal as it makes its purposeful way through the long line of 'Cheshire Locks'. All the locks were duplicated under the direction of Thomas Telford in the 1830s, though one or two have since been singled. Most peculiar of all, perhaps, was the rebuilding of one of the Thurlwood Locks in 1958. Subsidence from the adjacent salt works had brought Lock 53 to the brink of collapse, and so a new chamber was designed in the form of a steel tank supported by a series of piers which could be raised should further subsidence occur. Entry to the chamber was through guillotine gates. In practice the steel lock took longer to operate and was mistrusted by boatmen. It had been out of use for many years before demolition in 1987.

Another structure of significance was lost to the canalscape at Rode Heath where a large warehouse with arched loading bay stood beside the waterway until being controversially demolished in 1981. Hearing that the mill, a local landmark, was to be demolished, the Trent & Mersey

Canal Society successfully applied for the building to be given listed status. In response the mill's owners took the matter up with their local MP who managed to have protected status overturned. "After further consideration," quoted the DoE "we came to the conclusion that the building was not as interesting as at first thought."

Lawton Treble Locks are Telford's work and replaced a Brindley staircase which was both time consuming and wasteful of water. Beyond Church Locks there is a brief respite from the locks and the pleasant sight of Lawton church at the edge of woods surrounding Lawton Hall. Throughout this length the countryside dips and sweeps away from the canal in folds and creases like a carelessly discarded garment, revealing lush pastures interrupted by pockets of woodland through which footpaths beckon enticingly. Mow Cop (pronounced to rhyme with 'cow') overlooks this delightful landscape from its high ridge, an appropriate platform for the sober, yet lofty ambitions of the Primitive Methodists who held their first open air meeting on its summit in 1807. The castellated ruin, *continued overleaf:*

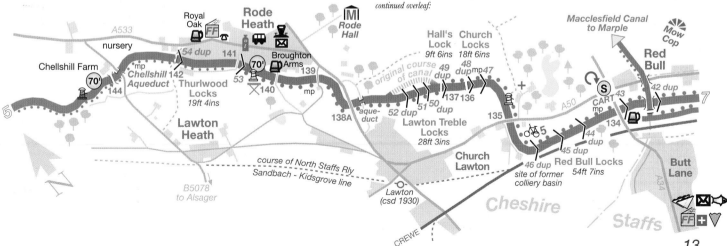

13

continued from page 13:

typical of 18th century romantic landscaping, is known as Wilbraham's Folly.

Red Bull Locks - once individually known as Townfield, Kent's and Yewtree in order of ascent - are probably the most visually satisfying on the whole of 'Heartbreak Hill'. All the elements are there by happy accident: a long, low stone wall separating the towpath from fields; the sweeping symmetries of the paired chambers masked from the railway by a high bank of beech trees; and an old whitewashed warehouse, once used for the storage of perishable goods, is now a facility centre for boaters.

Pool Lock Aqueduct seems weighed down by the responsibility of carrying the Macclesfield Canal over the Trent & Mersey. It is not an elegant work of engineering, but it's stood here for a hundred and eighty years and is no doubt good for a few more. Neither is the upper canal technically the 'Macclesfield', because it was the T&M themselves who built the Hall Green Branch, the Macclesfield Canal proper beginning at Hall Green stop lock one mile to the north beyond a second bridge, the Red Bull Aqueduct, which carries the canal over the A50 trunk road. The Macclesfield Canal is part of the popular "Cheshire Ring" canal circuit featured in another Pearson's Canal Companion. Southbound travellers along the Trent & Mersey, mystified by the Macclesfield's motive for crossing the T&M at this point, should turn to Map 7 for the exciting denouement.

Rode Heath   Map 6

Sizeable modern village at junction of A533 and A50. Two pubs vie for your custom: the Broughton Arms (Tel: 01270 878661 - ST7 3RU), canalside by Bridge 139, and the Royal Oak (Tel: 01270 875670 - ST7 3RU), reached from Bridge 142. Both are popular with boaters. There's also a Chinese takeaway called Jade Garden (Tel: 01270 873391), off licence and a well-stocked general store/post office. Buses run to and from the Potteries - Tel: 0871 200 2233.

Things to Do

RODE HALL - 18th century country house and gardens. Tel: 01270 873237. Open to the public on Wednesday and Bank Hol afternoons throughout the summer. Refreshments. Farmer's Market first Saturday morning of each month. ST7 3QP

Red Bull & Butt Lane   Map 6

RED BULL - Congleton Road (overlooking Lock 43). Tel: 01782 782600. Whitewashed without, cosy and welcoming inside, this southern outpost of Robinsons Brewery of Stockport offers a good choice of food lunchtimes and evenings. Reginald Mitchell, designer of the Spitfire fighter, was born nearby. ST7 3AJ

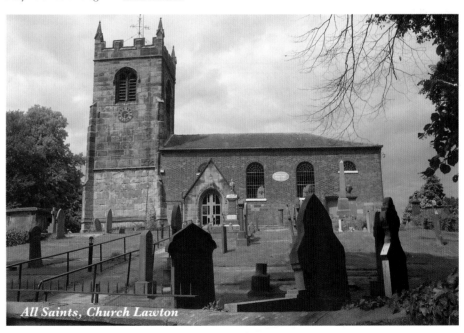

All Saints, Church Lawton

AT Hardings Wood the Trent & Mersey Canal makes a junction with the Macclesfield Canal. For southbound travellers the mysteries of Map 6 are enlightened. If, on the other hand, you have just emerged, still blinking, from Harecastle Tunnel, you may be baffled to find a canal, destined for the north, making its exit to the south. All will be revealed on Map 6.

Taking a boat through Harecastle Tunnel is one of the great inland waterway adventures. There is a tunnel keeper at either end responsible for controlling passage through the narrow bore. You may be delayed waiting for oncoming boats to clear the tunnel before the keeper gives you, and perhaps others going your way, instructions to enter. Gingerly you penetrate the gloom beyond the portal. Gradually all sense of light is lost. Nostalgically you look over your shoulder at the retreating half-moon of daylight. Suddenly, with a shuddering clang, the doors at the southern end close and the fume extractor fans begin to suck with a muted roar. For the next three-quarters of an hour you are buried deep beneath Harecastle Hill: with one small niggle at the back of your mind - will you or won't you come face to face with the 'Kidsgrove Bogart'?

The original tunnel through Harecastle Hill was designed by James Brindley. It took eleven years to build, was one and three-quarter miles long, and opened in 1777, five years after Brindley's death. A series of connecting tunnels led off the main bore to adjacent coal faces beneath Golden Hill, intersecting with several underground springs which provided additional water supplies to the summit level. A curious feature of this seepage occurs to this day, in that the water either side of the tunnel is tinted a peculiar orange shade by minute particles of ironstone rock.

For fifty years, teams of 'leggers' propelled boats through Brindley's towpathless tunnel, lying on their backs at right angles to the boat and literally 'walking' from one end to another, a feat which took two to three hours depending on the amount of alcohol consumed beforehand. Not surprisingly Harecastle became a serious traffic bottleneck. Reluctantly, being well aware of the costs and difficulties involved, the canal company commissioned a second bore with Thomas Telford as consultant engineer. Some idea of the advances in technology gained in the interim can be gauged from the fact that the new tunnel, equipped with a towpath, was completed in less than three years, opening in 1827.

Until the early years of the 20th century, the two tunnels were used in unison: Brindley's taking southbound boats, Telford's north. In 1914 electric tugs began to haul strings of boats through Telford's tunnel and Brindley's, now riddled with subsidence, was abandoned. The tugs were curious machines, unique on our waterways. They dragged themselves along a steel cable laid on the canal bed, collecting power through a tram-like pole from an overhead cable. They successfully solved Harecastle's traffic flow problems into the 1950s, by which time the number of boats using the tunnel had diminished so as to render them unviable. In 1954 forced ventilation was introduced, enabling powered boats to pass through, a system still in use today. Further subsidence caused

continued overleaf:

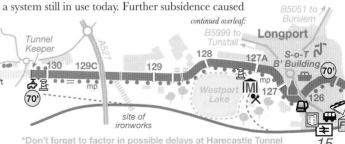

COUNTIES RING

Kidsgrove

Tesco

Harecastle Tunnel timetable
- see page 93

Harecastle Tunnel
2926 yards

Kidswood

Boathorse Road

Tunnel Keeper

Longport
B5051 to Burslem
B5999 to Tunstall

S-o-T
B' Building

airshaft   airshaft

Boathorse Road

airshaft

Westport Lake

site of ironworks

Hardings Wood Junction

Tunnel Keeper

Ravenscliffe

for details of facilities at Kidsgrove and Longport turn to page 16

Don't forget to factor in possible delays at Harecastle Tunnel

15

continued from page 15:

closure of the tunnel between 1973-77, but a good deal of money has been spent on its rehabilitation and it is now in excellent condition.

Refurbishment of the tunnel involved removal of the towpath, so walkers are faced with the option of catching a local train between Kidsgrove and Longport, or following the old boathorse route across the top, encountering the arcane, unvisited landscape of Harecastle Hill which Brindley and Telford must have been familiar with. Nearing the hilltop, the lane becomes more potholed, bounded with rough pasture grazed by unkempt ponies. An abattoir and traveller's camp intervene, whilst there are breathtaking views encompassing Jodrell Bank, the Wedgwood (not *that* Wedgwood, another one altogether) monument and the exciting urban panorama of the Potteries. In fact, all things considered, this is an adventure every bit as exciting as the boater's rite of passage underground. Incidentally, when the railway came to be built beneath Harecastle Hill it required three tunnels, two of which were abandoned when the line was electrified in 1966.

Between Harecastle's southern portal and Longport, the canal runs along its 408ft summit at the foot of a ridge supporting Tunstall, northern-most of the six Potteries towns. Industry once thronged the cut, but there is an air of desolation here now. From Bridge 129 to 130 the vast Ravensdale ironworks framed the canal, as massive in its heyday as Shelton Bar, three miles to the south. Today, though, no trace remains at all. Indeed the only action is provided by cars and lorries thundering across the Tunstall by-pass, completed late in 1998 and recently numbered (rather bizarrely) as Bridge 129C. Nevertheless, for the industrial archaeologist the adrenalin will be flowing. Look out for Copp Lane canal cottages by Bridge 129, the ruined edge of the side bridge which spanned the ironworks arm, and the stubs of old basins where the gasworks stood by Bridge 128 and where Josiah Wedgwood reputedly cut the canal's first sod.

Westport Lake has traditionally been a resort for Potteries folk lacking the time or the wherewithal to reach Rhyl or Blackpool, the seaside towns traditionally favoured by the area's inhabitants. The lake remains an attraction, enhanced recently, by the building of a new Visitor Centre by the Staffordshire Wildlife Trust, an establishment whose cafe offers such good views across the water that you could kid yourself it's Lake Como.

At Longport, some of the traditional aspects of North Staffordshire make their presence felt. A fine example of the once ubiquitous bottle kiln looms over the canal by Bridge 125. The buildings at Longport Wharf once belonged to the Mersey, Weaver & Ship Canal Carrying Co., one of the region's pre-eminent canal carrying concerns, many of whose vessels were built at the dock here in Longport. In their heyday, Mersey Weaver flyboats offered a 48-hour service between Liverpool and Stoke, including transhipment at Anderton. Steelite present the contemporary face of Potteries industry, within their modern premises they make china and glassware.

Kidsgrove   Map 7

A former colliery town on the wrong side of Harecastle Hill to qualify as a member of that exclusive hell-fire club called The Potteries. Its initially foreboding air thaws on closer acquaintance. A path leads up from the tunnel mouth to St Thomas's, "the bargee's church", and there are signposted ways through nearby "Kidswood". James Brindley is buried at Newchapel, a couple of miles to the east.

Eating & Drinking

BLUE BELL - adjacent Lock 41. Tel: 01782 774052. *Good Beer Guide* recommended pub prized for its ever changing cycle of real ales. ST7 1EG

Shopping

Tesco supermarket, butchers, bakers and branches of the main banks and a launderette. Make it your goal to find Kidsgrove Oatcakes on King Street where you can watch oatcakes and pikelets being freshly made on the griddle, and have your oatcakes crammed with a choice of nourishing fillings; Wrights pies and baps also available. Calor gas, diesel and solid fuel are obtainable from Smithsons by Bridge 132. Tel: 01782 787887.

Connections

TRAINS - hourly services to/from Longport and Stoke useful for towpath/tunnel top walkers and/or claustrophobics Tel: 08457 484950.

TAXIS - Tel: 01782 775775.

Longport   Map 7

All the 'ports' - Long, Middle, West and New - lie down in the valley beside the canal and the origin of their names is obvious, forming as they do, a necklace of wharfingering communities where the import and export of cargoes of The Potteries were handled. Longport, lying as it does on an incredibly busy link road with the A500, makes few concessions in appearance. Lorries thunder through leaving a tidemark halfway up the fronts of shops where merchandising and point of sale are alien jargon.

BUSES - frequent services up the hill to Burslem - Tel: 0871 200 2233.

TRAINS - as per Kidsgrove.

8 TRENT & MERSEY Etruria & Stoke 4mls/5lks/3hrs*

T HE Trent & Mersey Canal plunges through the heart of the manufacturing district it was built primarily to serve - a heart, however, broken time and time again as the age of coal gave way to the age of the computer. Until 1978 the canal penetrated the torrid core of Shelton Bar steel-works, scene of H. G. Wells' terrifying short story, *The Cone*, in which the steelmaster murders his wife's would-be lover by pushing him into a furnace. For a couple of decades thereafter only a rolling mill remained in use, though canal travellers were required to pass through the gloom of two overhanging fabrication sheds. In 2000 the plant closed, and has been

obliterated: no longer do you wave at the shunting engine drivers; no longer do the steelworkers cross the canal on their way back to Burslem at the end of a shift. In time some new development will probably rise phoenix-like from the rubble: sleek, shimmering and devoid of all character.

The derelict acres left behind after demolition of the blast furnaces became the site of the 1986 National Garden Festival, subsequently developed into the Festival Park, a ubiquitous mix of leisure, retail and commercial facilities. Such transformations are not without irony. Centrepiece of Festival Park is an hotel converted from Josiah Wedgwood's original Etruria Hall built on a

continued overleaf:

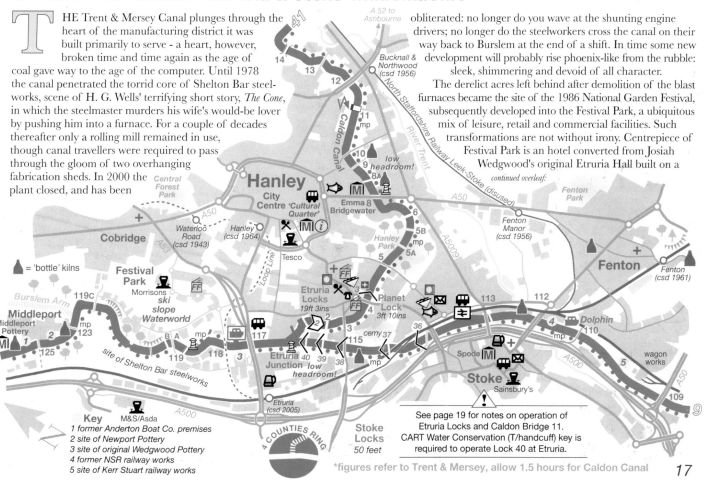

Key
1 former Anderton Boat Co. premises
2 site of Newport Pottery
3 site of original Wedgwood Pottery
4 former NSR railway works
5 site of Kerr Stuart railway works

See page 19 for notes on operation of Etruria Locks and Caldon Bridge 11. CART Water Conservation (T/handcuff) key is required to operate Lock 40 at Etruria.

*figures refer to Trent & Mersey, allow 1.5 hours for Caldon Canal

continued from page 17:

green-field site contemporary with the canal. During the 19th century the steelworks had encroached on the mansion, gradually engulfing its landscaped grounds. So, in a way, the developments of the 1980s returned the neighbourhood to its origins. Anyone familiar with the canal prior to the shutdown of Shelton Bar, however, is bound to mourn the lost drama associated with boating through the cacophonous and acrid plant.

Like many heavily industrialised regions, The Potteries have passed through a period of transition; though here, perhaps, the pace of change has been less relentless, and something of the old atmosphere is still tangible. From time to time you come upon examples of the area's most potent symbol, the bottle kiln. There was a time, before the Clean Air Act, when visitors could purchase postcards depicting The Potteries' skyline blackened by the combined emissions from serried ranks of these ovens.

For reasons never convincingly explained, Arnold Bennett - who is to The Potteries as Hardy to Wessex or Lawrence to Nottinghamshire - always referred to just 'Five Towns' in his prolific novels and short stories which portray the area around the turn of the 19th/20th centuries. He wrote that the Five Towns could never be described adequately because Dante had lived too soon. Inferno or not, five towns or six, there was always, and still to some extent is, a proud independence and individualism about The Potteries which sets it apart on an island between the Midlands and the North. Notice how the local accent has more in common with Merseyside than Manchester: could this have something to do with the

development of the Trent & Mersey and the associations it prospered?

Between Middleport and Etruria the canal twists and turns frequently, following the contours of the valley of the Fowlea Brook. Middleport Pottery (revitalised by the Prince's Regeneration Trust) evokes all the hallmarks of a traditional pottery, though its bottle kiln is the only survivor of seven which once stood shoulder to shoulder on the site. This is where Burleigh's time-honoured pottery is manufactured and offside moorings are provided for visitors. Next door stands the terracotta gabled end of the Anderton Boat Company's former warehouse, a well known carrier in the district whose boats were nicknamed 'knobsticks'. The premises are now occupied by William Edwards, designers of bespoke bone china.

Near Bridge 125, on a site now occupied by modern housing, stood Newport Pottery, famous for its connections with Clarice Cliff, the celebrated creator of 'Bizarre' and other Art Deco ceramics and pottery designs. By Bridge 123 an arm once led to Burslem Wharf, scene of the pantechnicon's immersion in Bennett's hilarious novel, *The Card*. The arm was abandoned in 1961 after a breach, but there have been proposals that it could be reinstated for moorings, and work parties have begun to clear debris.

Nowadays inscrutable call centres border the canal, but here and there are clues to a more colourful past: a boat dock beneath a roving bridge and another bridge (118) where the 'Loop Line' railway once weaved its way from one Six Towns community to the next. A wooden, windlass-operated lift bridge frames entry to the Festival Park Marina where secure moorings are available for an overnight stop and the chance to indulge in all the spurious activities modern life offers: supermarkets, ski slopes, swimming pools with wave machines, ten pin bowling alleys, fast food outlets and cinemas. Wedgwood's pottery stood opposite before subsidence and pollution forced the company to move to Barlaston (Map 9). All that remains is an enigmatic roundhouse, one of a pair which fronted the works.

Etruria Junction has all the ingredients of a compelling canalscape, much of its surviving charm emanating from the juxtaposition of the two, uppermost locks of the Stoke Five (the uppermost of which was formerly roofed over) and the handsomely constructed and resonantly named Etruscan Bone Mill which stands alongside a small arm issuing from the tail of the second lock down. The Bone mill now houses an industrial museum, the entrance to which is beside the Caldon Canal and overlooked

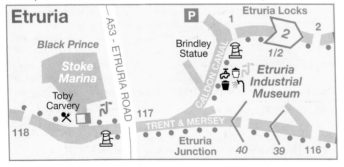

by a statue of Brindley, appearing rather more svelte, it must be said, than he does at Coventry Basin. Etruria's busy basin did not always deal solely in goods. In the 1840s, during a recession in the pottery trade, large numbers of emigrants began a long, life-changing journey aboard narrowboats from this wharf, destined for Wisconsin in North America, where a township named Pottersville was established.

Southwards from Etruria, the Trent & Mersey negotiates Stoke Locks, a fascinating flight, brim-full of images jostling for your attention: a ruined flour mill; a cemetery providing a splash of green in a sea of otherwise grey industry; a pair of bottle ovens (engulfed now by a housing scheme); a railway siding where tank wagons discharge china clay (a vital commodity which would once have been brought round the coast from Cornwall to the Mersey and transhipped into narrowboats for the journey down to The Potteries) and the bottom lock in the flight, deep and concrete lined, a rebuilding dating from construction of the adjacent Queensway, itself again rebuilt in recent times to cope with ever increasing road traffic.

By Bridge 113, the Newcastle-under-Lyme Canal once diverged from the main line. Opened in 1798, it ran in a V shape for 4 miles to the nearby borough of that name which, curiously, already had a canal. The Sir Nigel Gresley Canal, a three mile private waterway unconnected with any other canals, had opened in 1775 to carry coal from outlying collieries belonging to the Gresley family into Newcastle itself. The Newcastle Junction Canal was subsequently built to link the two canals, but an inclined plane, planned to bridge the disparity in height between the two 'Newcastle' canals, was never constructed. Stoke Boat Club used the first few hundred yards of the canal as moorings in the nineteen-sixties.

Crossing the tiny Trent, little evidence remains of Kerr Stuart's locomotive works where L. T. C. Rolt served an apprenticeship for three years from 1928. He writes vividly about his days in Stoke in *Landscape With Machines*, his first volume of autobiography. Happily a tradition of railway engineering continues in the shape of a modern rolling stock works. On the opposite bank of the canal, across the A500, is the site of Stoke City's former Victoria Ground, demolished when the club moved to their new Britannia Stadium, just along the cut.

The Caldon Canal

Inland navigators, setting off from Etruria on the thirty mile trip to Uttoxeter, implied by the milepost at the junction, are in for a disappointment. They can travel for seventeen miles to the remote wharf at Froghall, hidden deep in the woodlands of the Churnet Valley, but the canal onwards from that point to Uttoxeter was filled in and converted into a railway a century and a half ago. Nevertheless, the Caldon is one of the most delightful waterways in England, a thing of rare beauty, all the more enchanting because it is unfathomably under-utilised.

From Etruria the Caldon Canal immediately declares its intentions, ascending Etruria (aka Bedford Street) staircase locks, followed by another single lock (Planet) as it skirts Hanley, chief of the Six Towns. Dipping through an overbridge, it runs beside a stone wall over which peeps a typical Northern terrace. This simple throwback explains eloquently enough the inherent pathos of The Potteries: backyards with rainwater tubs and washing-lines; cobbled alleyways patrolled by stray dogs; net curtains blown softly by draughts unhampered by double-glazing. In another place, not far to the North, you would immediately think of Lowry or Coronation Street. But these are The Potteries, as warming, full of flavour, and insusceptible to the march of time as a Wrights steak & kidney pie.

Beyond Planet Lock the canal bisects Hanley Park, passing beneath a series of ornamental bridges. From a balcony embellished with terracotta, steps climb to a clock-towered pavilion from which you half expect Arnold Bennett characters to emerge at any moment: or, at least, we used to, before the pavilion was boarded-up. Come on council, *find* a use for it.

Then follows a zone of redevelopment, where pottery works are in retreat, faced with a vanguard of new housing. When we first covered this route in the mid 1980s boats carrying crockery worked out as far as Milton. Time was money and they didn't hang about. When you encountered one it was invariably accompanied by a tidal wave. *continued on Map 41, page 74*

⚠ Etruria (aka Bedford Street) Locks are a 'staircase' pair, but differ from most of their type in that an overflow weir permits the top chamber to be emptied into the lower chamber even when full. Ivy House Lift Bridge (11) on the Caldon Canal is electrified and requires a CART facilities key. The barriers are now operated by the push button controls, a big improvement!

Hanley
Map 8

Arnold Bennett called his 'Hanbridge' the Chicago of the Five Towns, which was his way of clarifying the confusing situation whereby it is Hanley that is the commercial heart of Stoke-on-Trent. Stoke is just one of the six communities, along with Tunstall, Burslem, Hanley itself, Longton and Fenton, that were merged to form Britain's fourteenth largest city in 1910. In any case the people of The Potteries have never been enamoured with the concept of belonging to an amorphous whole, preferring to shelter within the proudly individual characters of the six constituent towns. Hanley has suffered most from the pressures of the Consumer Age, and development has exorcised a good deal of the previously entrenched atmosphere of dignified northern provincialism. Heavens above, there is even a 'cultural quarter' now, something that would have Bennett choking on his Parisian cocktail.

Eating & Drinking
HOLY INADEQUATE - Etruria Old Road (west of Bridge 118). Tel: 0777 135 8238. Real ale and locally sourced pork pies. *Good Beer Guide* entry. ST1 5PL
MIRCHI - Snow Hill, Shelton (just up from Bridge 4 on the Caldon Canal). Tel: 01782 284488. Warmly regarded Indian restaurant and take-away open from 5pm daily (noon Sat & Sun). ST1 4LY
PORTOFINO - Marsh Street South. Tel: 01782 209444. Stylish Italian in the centre of Hanley. ST1 1JD
The Potteries are not well endowed with eating places, though there are a Toby Carvery and Frank & Bennys at Festival Park, whilst the cafes at Middleport and Emma Bridgewater potteries are exemplars of their ilk.

Shopping
All facilities are available in the centre of Hanley which is about 15 minutes walk from the Trent & Mersey Canal at Etruria, but less distant from the Caldon Canal at Bridges 4 or 8. Frequent buses run from stops on Bridge 117. The Potteries Centre houses all the usual chain stores, whilst the Market Hall provides an outlet for local retailing. North Staffordshire delicacies include 'oatcakes' and 'pikelets'; whilst Wrights have a number of shops and stalls selling their popular meat pies etc. On Tontine Street is Webberleys excellent independent bookshop and an interesting selection of local titles. Should you need a supermarket shop, Morrisons are located in Festival Park, whilst there's a massive Tesco 'Extra' reasonably close to the canal at Etruria.

Things to Do
TOURIST INFORMATION CENTRE - Museum & Art Gallery, Bethesda Street. Tel: 01782 236000. ST1 3DW
EMMA BRIDGEWATER - Lichfield Street. Tel: 01782 201328. Tours, shop & cafe. Mooring rings on the towpath above Bridge 8 on the Caldon Canal. ST1 3EJ
ETRURIA INDUSTRIAL MUSEUM - canalside Bridge 116 (entrance beside the Caldon Canal). Admission charge. Tel: 0790 026 7711. Cafe and small shop. Restored potters mill of exceptional interest. The mill dates from 1857 and was built to grind animal bones for use in 'bone' china. Open selected days. ST1 4RB
MIDDLEPORT POTTERY - Port Street, Burslem (between bridges 125 & 126). Tel: 01782 499766. Manufacturers of Burleigh ware. Tours, museum, shop & cafe. Open 10am-4pm. Visitor Moorings. ST6 3PE
POTTERIES MUSEUM & ART GALLERY - Bethesda Street, Hanley. Tel: 01782 232323. Open 10am-5pm (11am-4pm Sun), admission free. Features the Staffordshire Hoard, ceramics, a section devoted to local man Reginald Mitchell's Spitfire fighter plane, and a rich collection of drawings, paintings and prints. Small displays celebrating Arnold Bennett and the native composer Havergal Brian. ST1 3DW
SPODE - Elenora Street, Stoke. Tel: 01782 844718. Open Mar-Nov Fri-Sun. Archive material relating to this once famous brand. Demonstrations and sales. ST4 1QQ
TRENTHAM ESTATE - Stone Road (approx a mile west of Bridge 106, Map 9) Tel: 01782 646646. Hugeley popular regeneration of the old Sutherland estate. Gardens, woodlands, shopping, eating, monkeys. ST4 8JG

Connections
BUSES - services throughout The Potteries. Tel: 0871 200 2233. TAXIS - City Cabs. Tel: 01782 844444.

Stoke
Map 8

Known as 'Knype' in Arnold Bennett's stories, Stoke was, and still is, the railhead for The Potteries. Here, his Five Towns characters waited for the old Loop Line trains to take them to 'Hanbridge' (Hanley), 'Bleakridge' (Cobridge) and 'Bursley' (Burslem). The station itself (east of the canal) is a sort of Jacobean mansion with platforms where you might otherwise expect to find the croquet lawn. Across Winton Square, with its statue of Josiah Wedgwood, stands an equally imposing hotel. West of the canal (across Queensway) the town itself is somewhat lacklustre, only the Classical Town Hall and Minster Church of St Peter-ad-Vincula make any architectural impact, though the tombs of Wedgwood and Spode lie in the latter's capacious and arboreal churchyard.

Eating & Drinking
GLEBE - Glebe St. W of Br 113. Tel: 01782 860670. Joule's pub open from noon daily. Beautiful early 19c interior. Lunches Mon-Sat, dinners Tue-Sat. ST4 1HG

Connections
TRAINS - major railhead near Bridge 113. Local trains to Longport etc. Tel: 08457 484950.

Barlaston
Map 9

Suburban enclave with a useful row of shops west of the canal and a convenience store/PO to the east.

Eating & Drinking
PLUME OF FEATHERS - Station Rd. (Bridge 103). Tel: 01782 373100. Open daily from 11am, this refurbished pub is owned by the actor Neil Morrissey. ST12 9DH

Things to Do
WEDGWOOD - adjacent Bridge 104. Tel: 01782 282986. Visitor centre re-opened mid 2015 after a £34m makeover. Tours, museum, shop, and refreshments served on Wedgwood china. ST12 9ER

EVERY city has its soft underbellys of suburbia, and Hem Heath is one of Stoke's; more so now that its colliery has been closed and razed to the ground. Following privatisation of the coal industry, there was a brave attempt to reopen the mine, though sadly this just postponed the inevitable. It's cheaper, it would appear, to buy coal from Australia nowadays than dig for it locally. Britannia Stadium has been Stoke City's home since 1997. Stanley Matthew's ashes are buried beneath the centre spot.

Blue brick abutments mark the course of the Trentham branch railway which, in its brief heyday, carried hordes of North Staffordshire day-trippers to the gardens of Trentham Hall. Trentham had been the seat of the Dukes of Sutherland, the most recent property having been completed in 1842 to the designs of Sir Charles Barry, architect of the Houses of Parliament. By all accounts it had been a most beautiful house set in the loveliest of landscaped parklands and Italian gardens. However, the Trent ran through these gorgeous grounds and, as the river grew more and more polluted by the combined effluents of The Potteries, life for the Duke, his household and visitors - which often included royalty - became less and less idyllic. Eventually the Duke was forced to quit Trentham for another of the family seats, and the hall was demolished just before the Great War. He left the grounds to the people of The Potteries and, as more sophisticated methods of sewage control were developed, Trentham Gardens became a celebrated resort for the residents of North Staffordshire. After a period in limbo, Trentham has been regenerated at considerable expense, and now once again features spectacular Italian Gardens. A tall monument commemorating the second Duke of Sutherland may be seen rising above woodlands to the west of Trentham Lock; as does one above the small coastal town of Golspie in Sutherland. Trentham Lock boasts a deep chamber with a pronounced undertow when filling. The foundations of its erstwhile keeper's cottage are readily apparent. Nearby stands the famous pottery works of Wedgwood. The company moved to Barlaston from their original site at Etruria in 1940.

The great Palladian facade of Barlaston Hall gazes benignly over the canal, a landmark case in the history of conservation. There were concerns that subsidence caused by mining at the former Hem Heath Colliery, which finally closed in the mid nineties, might bring about its demolition, but its future was redeemed by the pioneering conservation group SAVE and, fully restored, it has become a private home once more. Barlaston is a popular overnight mooring point - details of its amenities appear on Page 20. At one time there was a busy boatbuilding yard here. A row of cottages occupied by its workforce - now highly desirable properties indeed - may be observed on the offside south of Bridge 103.

⚠ Anti-vandal (handcuff) key required at Trentham Lock

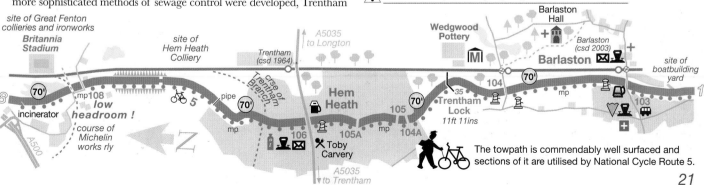

Trent & Mersey Canal

Salt Country

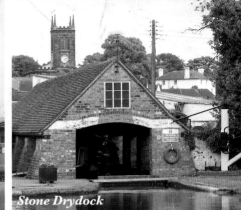

Stone Drydock

Essex Bridge

Harecastle

Saltersford Tunnel

Barnton Tunnel

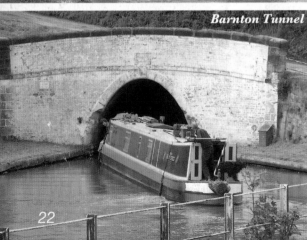

Etruria

Alrewas

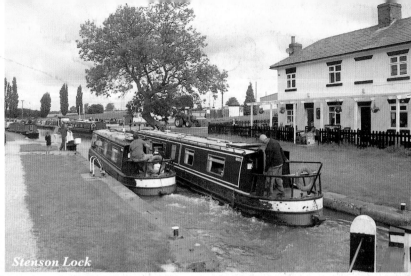
Stenson Lock

rmitage

Findern

23

MEAFORD Power Station is one of several along the Trent Valley demolished as the emphasis on the generation of electricity has shifted away from coal powered plants. There are four locks in the Meaford flight. Originally three of them were combined as a 'staircase'. Traces of the old course of the canal can clearly be seen to the west of the present layout. Meaford Locks form an attractive group (though in common with much of the Trent & Mersey's infrastructure and apparatus a pot or two of paint wouldn't go amiss) and are bordered by a country road with stone walling; one of the first signs that the North is beginning to give way to the Midlands, or vice versa. If you get into conversation with any locals it is disconcerting to hear them pronounce the place as 'Method'.

Making its way through the upper valley of the Trent, the canal encounters the market town of Stone, original headquarters of the Trent & Mersey Canal Company, which probably explains why the local foundry of Rangeley & Dixon won the contract to cast the T&M's distinctive mileposts. The town lost its role as the administrative centre for the canal when it was bought out by the North Staffordshire Railway in 1846, but retained an extensive dockyard for maintenance purposes. Nowadays the emphasis is obviously on leisure use, and there is still much to see as you chug through the four locks of the Stone flight. The second lock down, called Newcastle Road, is overlooked by the large convent school of St Dominic's which was designed by Joseph Hansom, the man who invented the Hansom cab.

A boat horse tunnel leads underneath the road to a busy pound occupied by extensive linear moorings for private boats. Stone Boat Building boasts an excellent chandlery. Still quaintly signwritten, the former ale stores of Joule's Brewery border the canal before it widens by a fascinating spread of docks, covered and uncovered, wet and dry. These belong to the Canal Cruising Company, a pioneer of boating holidays on the canals, having been founded in 1948. It was here that L. T. C. Rolt's boat *Cressy*, of *Narrow Boat* immortality, met its end, being broken up and cremated after failing a survey in 1951. Yard Lock, located beside the boatyard, is the deepest of the flight. On the other side of the canal the town's former hospital - once a workhouse - has, rather ironically, been converted into prestige accommodation. By Bridge 94, an enigmatic female sculpture commemorates Christina Collins, who met an untimely end on the Trent & Mersey Canal in 1839.

Star Lock is the bottom chamber in the flight. The pub from which it derived the name dates from the 16th century. An old warehouse on the offside below Bridge 93 has been converted into retirement flats, whilst several new buildings have been erected beside it in a pleasingly harmonious style. The canal company's offices stood alongside the towpath at this point, though there is no evidence of these now. They were demolished after the war, having been used for many years as a chocolate factory. Arguably the best moorings for access to the town are provided here, alongside a sportsground and children's play area.

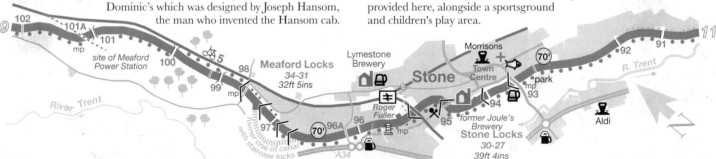

Stone

Map 10

Stone is a lively market town of some twelve thousand souls who display much affection for the canal on their doorstep. Conscious of their heritage, the local civic society have erected plaques on walls recalling that Peter de Wint, the landscape watercolourist, was born here; that the Duke of Cumberland came here to do battle; that the Star Inn has long attended to the thirst of passers-by; and that Henry Holland designed the bow-fronted Crown Inn in 1780. Stone has a history of brewing, Joule's and Bents being well-regarded far beyond the town's hinterland. Joule's - reinvented now in Market Drayton (see page 63) - began brewing in the town in 1758 and, with the advent of the canal, and the possibilities of export it brought, their ales became fashionable in Europe and the Americas. Once they operated a pair of boats to bring in coal for firing the steam plant. In 1970, however, they were absorbed into the Bass Charrington conglomerate and, hardly surprisingly, brewing ceased four years later; though the canalside ale stores remain intact. Bents, the town's other brewers, closed in the early 1960s, though bits of their brewery survive in industrial use, notably the micro-brewers Lymestone.

Eating & Drinking

BELLA NAPOLI - canalside Star Lock. Tel: 01785 817985. Lock-side Italian. open for lunch and dinner Mon-Fri and all day from noon Sat/Sun. ST15 8QW
BLUE ROOMS - Radford Street. Tel: 01785 819988. Bar and restaurant open Mon-Sat from 6pm. Famous for steaks, skillets and George's pies. ST15 8DA
THE BOREHOLE - Mount Road. Tel: 01785 817796. Lymestone's 'brewery tap'. Open daily from noon. Pork pies, baps and soup. A must for real ale fans. ST15 8LL
CULLENS - Radford Street. Tel: 01785 818925. Fine dining lunch & dinner daily ex Sun. ST15 8DA
GRANVILLES - Granville Square. Tel: 01785 816658. Brasserie and music bar with the emphasis on jazz. Open lunch & evening daily ex Sun. ST15 8AB

Christina Collins

THE OLIVES - Lichfield Street. Tel: 01785 813334. First floor Mediterranean restaurant open from 5pm daily. ST15 8QW
POSTE OF STONE - Granville Square. Tel: 01785 827920. Wetherspoons housed in former post office. Wide range of real ales and inexpensive meals with breakfasts being served from 8am. ST15 8AB
PRIORY FISH BAR - Lichfield Street. Tel: 01785 819992. Excellent fish & chip shop. ST15 8NA
ROYAL EXCHANGE - Radford Street. Tel: 01785 812685. *GBG* listed Titanic Brewery pub. ST15 8DA
THE STAR - canalside Bridge 93. Tel: 01785 813096. Quaint Marston's lockside pub serving a good range of food. ST15 8QW
SWAN INN - Lichfield Street (adjacent Bridge 93). Tel: 01785 815570. *Good Beer Guide* listed town centre local. Coach House ales from Warrington. ST15 8QW

Shopping

Stone is a good shopping centre with the advantage of being so close to the canal that you can easily carry heavy carrier-bags back to the boat. The annual Food & Drink Festival takes place in October. Fine stoneware and bone china from Dunoon on High Street. Co-op and Morrisons supermarkets. Market on Tuesdays, Fridays & Saturdays. Farmers Market on the 1st Saturday of each month. Whilst you can buy bottles of their beer from the farm shop at Aston Marina (Map 11), the Lymestone brewery itself occupies part of the former Bents Brewery on Mount Road beyond the railway station, and it is possible to purchase bottled beer, glasses etc direct from their Borehole micropub.

Connections

BUSES - Services to/from Stafford and Hanley. Tel: 0871 200 2233.
TRAINS - London Midland services connect Stone's handsome Jacobean station hourly with Stoke, Kidsgrove and Crewe in one direction and Stafford, Rugeley, Lichfield and London Euston in the other. Tel: 08457 484950.
TAXIS - K Cabs. Tel: 01785 288999.

TAKING apparent pleasure in each other's company, canal and river, road and railway make their undemonstrative way through a shallow valley, skirting, but scarcely encountering, a succession of small settlements, barely in the category of villages. With no great dramas to catch the eye, the canal traveller is thrown back on his own resources. He can pass the time wrestling with the great conundrums of life or anticipate the slow drawing of a foaming pint in the convivial bars of the Greyhound at Burston or the Dog & Doublet at Sandon.

Aston Lock marks the half-way point of the Trent & Mersey's route from Preston Brook to Shardlow; names which mean nothing now but were once as well known as Spaghetti Junction and Watford Gap. One of the distinctive cast iron mileposts, originally made in Stone by Rangeley & Dixon, quotes 46 miles in either direction. Aston Marina is one of the new breed of boating centres imaginatively offering more than just an aquatic car park. Burston is a well-kept secret, a beautiful small community idyllically grouped about a pond. The tiny church of St Rufin's, can trace its origins back to medieval times. An axle from Burston's former watermill is displayed on the green, recalling an era when communities like this worked rather than slumbered.

Between Aston and Burston a nature trail runs parallel to the canal, crossing farmland owned by Severn Trent water authority and chosen for experiments in biodiversity. Such technicalities apart, when combined with the canal towpath, the trail offers a delightful three mile circular walk. It's a short stroll from Sandon Lock to the picturesque village of the same name. Sandon Hall, home of the Harrowbys, is a Victorian house in Jacobean style, well hidden from the world in rolling parkland. Above the tree-line

peeps a slender urn-topped column commemorating William Pitt. Another Prime Minister, the assassinated Spencer Perceval, is recalled by a nearby shrine. Unfortunately the house and its grounds are only occasionally open to the public, but you can stroll eastwards and upwards along a lane which initially does an impression of Devon, but which by the time it has plateaued out thinks it is somewhere in the Scottish borders. Pheasants are busy being reared whilst the churchyard of All Saints dispenses panoramic views of the Trent Valley. Sadly its interior, replete with copious tombs and monuments, was locked on the occasion of our last visit. Other points of interest in Sandon include the war memorial at the crossroads, the quaint 'arts & crafts' style village hall and matching pub, and the ornate former station house, notable for the *porte-cochere*, built to accommodate the carriage from Sandon Hall.

Summary of Facilities

ASTON MARINA - Tel: 01785 819702. All the to-be-expected boater facilities (including pumpout and laundry) plus an exceptional butchery/food and drink outlet and a bistro with picturesque decking over the water and intriguing 'gazebos' for cosy assignations. ST15 8QU
There are two good country inns at Burston and Sandon: THE GREYHOUND (Tel: 01889 508263 - ST18 0DR) and DOG & DOUBLET (Tel: 01889 508331 - ST18 0DJ) respectively. Sandon also has a useful roadside stores.

G IVEN the great beauty of the countryside, it is no coincidence that several wealthy and influential families put down grandiose roots here. Built of brick and stone for the benefit of Sandon's gentry, Bridge 82 echoes the high aesthetic values of the 18th century.

Any scar tissue wrought by the advent of the canal must have been healed by the time the railways arrived. The North Staffordshire Railway followed the course of the Trent & Mersey (which it was soon to acquire) down the valley to Colwich and became a main line of some importance as a through route between Manchester and London via The Potteries. Another line arrived in the landscape, was absorbed into the Great Northern Railway and became a far-flung outpost of the LNER at the grouping of the railway companies in 1923. Passenger traffic was never significant - how could it be in these rural haunts? - but the milk of the Trent Valley's cows was creamy enough for the scheduling of a daily milk train to the capital. One activity in this otherwise rural area that the canal did help to prosper was the making of salt. The Trentside village of that name has associations with the trade going back to Medieval times; perhaps even Roman. But at both Shirleywich and Weston brine pumping developed significantly in the

18th Century because the canal was used to bring in coal to fuel evaporation and to carry away the finished product. Agriculture and industry combined to corner the market in salted beef for the Royal Navy, conveyed in barrels by narrow boat. Look out for the new canalside housing at Weston where the use of whitewashed brick gives the appearance of the properties concerned being much older.

Pasturefields Saltmarsh is an extremely rare - if not unique - example of an inland saltmarsh and provides an environment in which a number of halophytic, or salt tolerant, plants can thrive, amongst which are the charmingly named lesser sea spurrey and saltmarsh rue. Snipe, redshank and lapwing nest here too.

Summary of Facilities

The HOLLYBUSH INN at Salt (Tel: 01889 508234 - ST18 0BX) is an historic inn, highly regarded for its food. Weston offers two pubs: the SARACEN'S HEAD adjacent Bridge 80 (Tel: 01889 270286 - ST18 0HT) or THE WOOLPACK (Tel: 01889 270238 - ST18 0JH) which overlooks the village green. Alternatively you can stroll uphill to sample the Cellar Restaurant at 17th Century, mullion-windowed WESTON HALL (Tel: 01889 271082 - ST18 0BA).

With bicycles on board it's an easy detour to AMERTON FARM & CRAFT CENTRE (Tel: 01889 270294 - ST18 0LA) an eclectic mix of food and craft outlets with a tea room and a narrow gauge railway (weekends only) to boot. Buses to Stafford- Tel: 0871 200 2233.

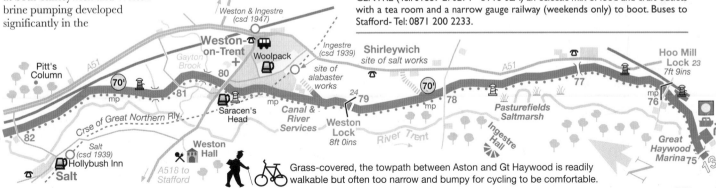

Grass-covered, the towpath between Aston and Gt Haywood is readily walkable but often too narrow and bumpy for cycling to be comfortable.

13 TRENT & MERSEY CANAL Great Haywood 4mls/11k/2hrs*

BRINDLEY invariably found it simpler to follow river valleys, and Great Haywood was an obvious choice of location for a canal junction designed to establish his scheme for a 'Grand Cross' of man made waterways linking the four great English estuaries: Humber, Thames, Severn and Mersey. With the completion of the Staffordshire & Worcestershire Canal in 1772, and the Trent & Mersey

five years later, Haywood became a canal junction of major importance, as significant to transport in the 18th century as any motorway interchange today. One is only left to marvel at the simplicity of it all - two quiet ribbons of water meeting beneath a bridge of exquisite beauty - and compare it wistfully with transport interchanges of the 21st century, acres of concrete, noise and pollution. Where did we go wrong? History may have taken some wrong turnings, but there is little chance for the canal traveller to make a mistake, for a prominent fingerpost directs one concisely enough to "Wolverhampton", "The Trent", or "The Potteries". Between here and Colwich the Trent & Mersey is at its most memorably beautiful as it skirts the boundary of Shugborough. On one bank beechwoods tumble down to the water's edge. On the other, across the Trent, there are glimpses of the statues, antiquities and follies which pepper the grounds of this famous

P Severn Springs

Cannock Chase

A513

River Trent

Colwich Lock 21
6ft 6ins

14

71
71A

72

Colwich
(csd 1958)

St Mary's Abbey

Little Haywood

Staffs Way

mp

Staffs Way

Triumphal Arch

P

M farm & mill

Tower of the Winds

Shugborough Hall & County Museum

Great Haywood

72A

Gt Haywood (csd 1947)

Essex Bridge

73 Haywood Lock 22
4ft 2ins

109   108

Haywood Junction

74   mp

4 COUNTIES RING

12

River Sow

Tixall Lock
4ft 3ins

43
107

106

aqueduct

Tixall Wide

Tixall

Tixall Gatehouse

P
FF
Milford & Brocton (csd 1950)

P Milford cricket ground

105 Milford

A513

104 Walton

103 Stone-ford

102

sewage works

23

N

Great Haywood

73

Essex Bridge

Haywood Lock

T & M   S & W

109   aqueducts

74

Anglo Welsh

Farm Shop

28

home of the Anson family. Colwich Lock lies in an attractive setting between the village church, a picturesque farm, and a bend in the river. From Bridge 72 you can take an idyllic walk to Severn Springs, a wonderful springboard for exploring Cannock Chase. Hidden from the canal, but visible from passing trains, St Mary's Abbey is occupied by a small order of Benedictine nuns who can trace their origins back to 17th Century France and an English order based in Cambrai.

The Staffordshire & Worcestershire Canal

Through the arch of Bridge 109 - an 18th century fusion of functional engineering and enduring loveliness - the Staffordshire & Worcestershire Canal commences its 46 mile journey down to the Severn at Stourport. Two aqueducts carry it across the Trent and a millstream. A couple of miles further on it crosses the Sow. Between these river crossings the canal suddenly casts off its inhibitions and widens into a broad lake of quite un-canal-like proportions, bordered by thick reedbeds inhabited by a gorgeous array of wildfowl. Boaters will find their craft looping the loop out of sheer exuberance. This is Tixall Wide or Broadwater and there are two theories for its surprising existence. Some maintain that the canal was widened into an artificial lake to placate the owner of Tixall Hall. Others that the expanse of water predates the canal, that it was naturally formed, and that Izaak Walton learnt to fish here. Whichever explanation suits you, don't miss the extraordinary Elizabethan gatehouse which overlooks the Wide. The hall itself, where Mary Queen of Scots was imprisoned for a fortnight in 1586, was demolished long ago. The gatehouse is let for holidays by the Landmark Trust who specialise in restoring and holiday-letting properties worth saving.

West of Tixall's solitary lock the canal meanders enchantingly through the valley of the Sow. A plethora of trees adds lustre to the landscape. The river is crossed by way of a typical low-slung Brindley masonry aqueduct. Bridge 105 is a handsome turnover affair from which there is access under the railway to the village of Milford and Cannock Chase. Between here and Baswich the canal runs through fields between the river and the railway whose southbound trains are quickly gobbled up by the decorated portal of Shugborough Tunnel. Those of a railway bent may be intrigued to learn that Francis William Webb, the great locomotive engineer of the London & North Western Railway, hailed from Tixall, where his father was Rector for over half a century. Sir Nigel Gresley, of *Flying Scotsman* and *Mallard* fame, also famously had a man of the cloth for a father.

The Haywoods   Map 13

The villages of Great and Little Haywood are separated by a long, high 'make-work' wall. Dormitory housing has inevitably expanded both populations, but the centres remain peaceful and largely unspoilt; especially so in the charming lane leading from Great Haywood, under the railway and over the canal, to the Essex Bridge, one of the finest examples of a packhorse bridge imaginable. Tolkien convalesced in Great Haywood after catching trench fever during the Battle of the Somme, and it is thinly disguised as 'Tavrobel' in *The Tale of The Sun and The Moon*. It is further suggested that the rivers Gruir and Afros, which feature in that story, were inspired by the Trent and Sow.

Eating & Drinking

CLIFFORD ARMS - Village centre. Tel: 01889 881321. *GBG* listed pub open from noon daily. ST18 0SR

LOCK HOUSE - adjacent Haywood Lock. Tel: 01889 881294. Canalside tea room/restaurant. ST18 0ST

Shopping

Little Haywood has a convenience store. Great Haywood has a pharmacy and convenience stores at either end of the village, the northernmost incorporating a butchers and post office. CANALSIDE FARM SHOP - Bridge 74. Tel: 01889 881747. Well stocked farm shop and cafe. ST18 0RQ

Things to Do

SHUGBOROUGH - access via Haywood Lock and Essex Bridge. Tel: 01889 881388. Open daily mid March to late October daily (ex Tuesdays) 11am-5pm. Admission charge. Attractions include mansion, county museum, working farm, watermill, gardens, shop and cafeteria. A visit to the farm can be particularly recommended for families. ST17 0XB

Connections

BUSES - Arriva service 825 operates half-hourly Mon-Sat (hourly Sun) between Stafford and Lichfield via Little Haywood. D & G service 841 links Gt. Haywood with Stafford and Uttoxeter (an interesting little town to visit) hourly Mon-Sat. Tel: 0871 200 2233.

Milford   Map 13

Traditionally a motorist's gateway to Shugborough and The Chase, Milford now has the benefit of a mountain bike hire facility (Mammoth - Tel: 01785 664555 ST17 0UR) should canallers feel the need to swap modes for a bit. Other facilities include the Barley Mow (a Greene King 'Eating-Inn' - Tel: 01785 662896 ST17 0UW) and The Viceroy (an Indian - Tel: 01785 663239 ST17 0UH) plus Britain's most long-lived Wimpy. The easiest access to all these facilities is along a track which leads beneath the railway from Bridge 105.

14 TRENT & MERSEY CANAL Colwich & Rugeley 4mls/0lks/1.5hrs

THE river's slow influence pervades the canal, and the pair wander across the landscape like indolent lovers on a long afternoon, chaperoned at a discreet distance by the recumbent mass of The Chase. Several big houses were built by prosperous landowners in this enchanting countryside. The stuccoed facade of Bishton Hall overlooks the canal. Nowadays it is a prep school with an idyllic cricket ground shaded by ancient chestnut trees bordering the water. Intriguingly, it once featured a Grecian boathouse on the banks of the Trent, the remains of which can be found amidst the undergrowth on the riverbank by a spill-weir. Another mansion, Wolseley Hall, stood opposite on the far bank of the river. It was demolished long ago, but the grounds have been incorporated into the Staffordshire Wildlife Trust's Wolseley Centre. Wolseley Bridge has graced the Trent here since 1800. It was designed by John Rennie, best known in canal circles for his work on the Kennet & Avon.

The towpath plays host to a pair of walking routes: the Staffordshire Way (Mow Cop to Kinver) and Millennium Way (Newport to Burton-on-Trent). Rugeley usually gets a bad press from guidebooks, but we have always had a soft spot for this down to earth little town, once home to the notorious Victorian poisoner, William Palmer and also remembered as the scene, in 1839, of the canal murder of Christina Collins. In years gone by Rugeley was the site of a malodorous tannery (where flats have been built at Bridge 66) but it is the power station which dominates now, being opened here in the Sixties to take advantage of coal mined on the spot; though the colliery has closed and nowadays coal is brought in by train from far and wide - often having originated beyond these shores.

At Brindley Bank the canal suddenly stops running parallel with the Trent and turns sharply to cross it, as though Brindley had been screwing up his courage to bridge the river. Once there was a transhipment wharf here where flint was swapped between canal and river vessels for the short run down to Colton Mill by Trent Valley railway station. A handsome pumping station overlooks this crossing of water over water, though the aqueduct itself is of little aesthetic appeal. By Bridge 68 a short, reedy arm adjacent to the railway provides a useful turning point for lengthy craft. This may have been used as a transhipment basin in the fledgling days of the railway, perhaps for the conveyance of building materials.

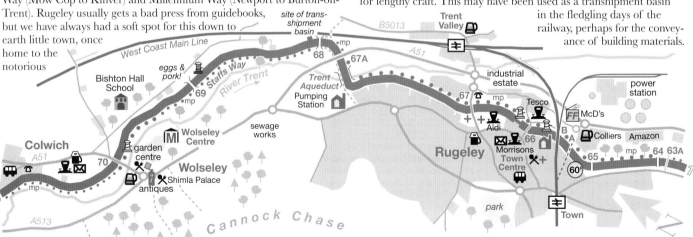

Wolseley Bridge
Map 14

Wolseley has a craft centre, antiques showroom, art gallery, wine merchant and garden centre (with cafe/restaurant) all accessible from Bridge 70.

Eating & Drinking
WOLSELEY ARMS - far side of river bridge. Tel: 01889 883179. Vintage Inns establishment, once the meeting place for the canal's promoters. ST17 0XS
SHIMLA PALACE - far side of river bridge by roundabout. Tel: 01889 881325. Indian restaurant, eat in or takeaway. ST17 0XS

Things to Do
THE WOLSELEY CENTRE - Wolseley Bridge (far side of river bridge beyond roundabout). Tel: 01889 880100. Staffordshire Wildlife Trust headquarters set in revitalised 26 acre garden park. ST17 0WT

Connections
BUSES - Arriva service 825 as per Rugeley.

Rugeley
Map 14

A former mining town well versed in the vicissitudes of existence following the abandonment of the local pit in 1990. Scots accents are occasionally to be heard, immigrants who came to work in the mine and remained washed-up by its closure. It is difficult to escape the impression that life here is lived on the cheap - though not without a certain deadpan dignity. Here in the tight-knit streets, and on the old Coal Board estates, one finds thrift and graft and a perverse civic pride, whilst a consoling beauty is to be found up on the nearby Chase. In the churchyard of St Augustine's (adjacent Bridge 67) an isolated gravestone remembers Christina Collins, noting that 'having been most barbarously treated was found dead in the Canal in this parish on 17th June 1839'. The story behind her misadventure - for which two boatmen were hung publicly at Stafford Gaol - inspired Colin Dexter's Inspector Morse story *The Wench is Dead*.

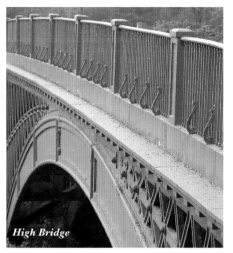
High Bridge

Eating & Drinking
PLAZA - Horsefair. Tel: 01889 586831. Wetherspoons characteristically housed in former cinema. WS15 2EJ
TERRAZZA - Lichfield Street. Tel: 01889 570630. Italian open Tue-Sat from 6.30pm. WS15 2EH
THE COLLIERS - Power Station Road (adjacent Bridge 66A). Tel: 01889 503951. Table Table bar/restaurant open for breakfast from 6.30am (7am weekends); main meals from noon 'til late. WS15 1LX

Shopping
Moor north of Bridge 66 for easiest access to town centre. Morrisons, Tesco and Aldi supermarkets. Market Hall and outdoor markets on Tue, Thur, Fri & Sat.

Connections
BUSES - Arriva service 825 (half-hourly Mon-Sat, hourly Sun) links Rugeley with Stafford (via Wolseley) and Lichfield (via Armitage and Handsacre) and is thus ideal for one-way towpath walks. Tel: 0871 200 2233.

TRAINS - useful hourly London Midland service along the Trent Valley and hourly from Town or Trent Valley stations to Cannock (a pretty quarter of an hour's ride away up over the flanks of the Chase), Walsall and Birmingham. Tel: 08457 484950.

TAXIS - Town & Country. Tel: 01889 576621.

Handsacre
Map 15

The High Bridge spanning the Trent to the north of Bridge 58 is well worth a sortie ashore. Its graceful cast-iron arch was made at Coalbrookdale in 1830.

Eating & Drinking
THE CROWN - canalside Bridge 58. Tel: 01543 490239. Refurbished pub. WS15 4DT
THE OLD PECULIER - village centre. Cosy local. Tel: 01543 491891. WS15 4DP
MICHAEL'S - The Green. Tel: 01543 491314. Lengthy queues for great fish & chips. WS15 4DT

Shopping
Convenience store and newsagent.

Connections
BUSES - Arriva service 825 as per Rugeley.

Armitage
Map 15

Offside moorings provide access via an alleyway to a goodly number of shops on the main road.

Eating & Drinking
PLUM PUDDING - canalside Bridge 61A. Tel: 01543 490330. Former canalside pub currently operating as an Italian restaurant 'Il Marchigiano'. WS15 4AZ
SPODE COTTAGE - across road from above. Tel: 01543 490353. Bar/restaurant. WS15 4AT
ASH TREE - canalside Bridge 62. Tel: 01889 578314. Marston's 'Two for One'. WS15 1PF

Shopping
Butcher, baker, post office, pharmacy, convenience store.

Connections
BUSES - Arriva service 825 as per Rugeley.

15 TRENT & MERSEY CANAL Armitage & Handsacre 4mls/0lks/1hr

WHILST by no means a length of canal likely to endear itself to connoisseurs of the picturesque, this stretch of the Trent & Mersey is never actually overwhelmed by industry, and there are a number of invigorating views over the Trent Valley or up on to the flanks of Cannock Chase.

The characteristic Trent & Mersey mileposts measure your progress, more relevant perhaps to the perspiring towpath walker than the languorous boater, laid-back on their tiller. They were put in place originally to facilitate the calculation of tolls, but at the outset of the Second World War, in common with most of Britain's road and railway signs, they were removed to befuddle invading Aryans. Remarkably, following a commendable campaign by the Trent & Mersey Canal Society in the 1970s, they have all been returned to their rightful places. The originals bear the inscription 'R&D Stone 1819', the replicas cast to replace those which had 'disappeared' during the interim, are inscribed 'T&MCS 1977'.

Armitage and Shanks are synonymous with toilet plumbing. Their trade marks are emblazoned on public conveniences throughout the world. Once they were separate firms, merging in 1969, but the site alongside the canal at Armitage dates back to 1817. Sanitaryware became a speciality in the 19th century under the management of Edward Johns - the origin of the Americanism "Going to the John". Today the factory, towering over a narrow stretch of canal spanned by the recently quadrupled West Coast Main Line railway, is huge and convincingly prosperous, and Ideal Standard -

as they are now somewhat less resonantly known - are a public limited company with a seemingly 'watertight' future.

Connections are apparent with another famous earthenware firm at Spode House and Hawkesyard Priory. Josiah Spode, a member of the North Staffordshire pottery family, left his house to a Dominican Order in 1893 and the monks proceeded to build a priory in the grounds, completing the work just prior to the First World War. The priory is now a conference centre, wedding venue and golf course.

Armitage's church is perched above a sandstone bluff by Bridge 61. Though much rebuilt by the Victorians, it retains its highly decorated Norman font. A path worth taking leads beneath the railway and over the Trent to the isolated settlement of Mavesyn Ridware which also has an interesting church. Occasionally, whether travelling on foot or afloat, you just feel the urge to turn your back on the canal.

Passing beneath the A513, the canal narrows and negotiates a rocky cutting. One-way working is the order of the day. This was formerly the site of Armitage (or "Plum Pudding") Tunnel, a dramatic unlined bore through the rock face. Subsidence, induced by coal mining, necessitated opening out of the tunnel, and concrete lining of the canal banks.

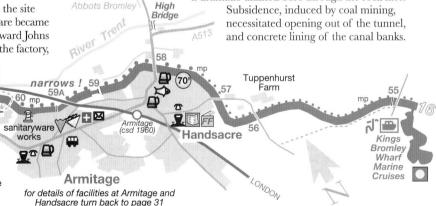

for details of facilities at Armitage and Handsacre turn back to page 31

A bend in the canal south of Woodend Lock, and glimpses of the three spires of Lichfield Cathedral, tell you that you and the Trent & Mersey have travelled as far south as you are ever going to get in the canal's arc-like journey between Preston Brook and Shardlow. Ravenshaw Woods are a riot of rhododendron colour in early summer. The works by Bridge 54 was once the smelly "milk factory" referred to by L. T. C. Rolt in *Narrow Boat*.

HS2 - on its way north from Birmingham to Manchester - controversially threatened to cross the canal at Fradley three times, but it would appear that the Inland Waterways Association, and other interested parties, have persuaded the new railway's engineers that once will be quite enough.

On hot summer days the junction is hugely popular with sightseers, but on winter afternoons it isn't difficult to imagine how it must have looked in the latter days of cargo carrying. Listening posts offer entertaining insights into Fradley's heritage. The Coventry Canal heads off in a southerly direction towards Fazeley and Tamworth - a route covered in the "South Midlands" and "Stourport Ring" Canal Companions. A popular cafe occupies part of the T&M's maintenance yard. On the opposite bank

private woodland masks Fradley Pool, which, in recent years, has been opened out as a visitor attraction with bird hides and facilities for pond dipping. The Trent & Mersey constructed a channel from just above Middle Lock to feed the reservoir as a means of ensuring that their valuable supplies weren't diverted into the Coventry Canal.

Between Fradley and Alrewas the canal crosses former common land and the flat nature of the adjoining fields engenders a distinct feeling of emptiness. The canal curves endearingly through the picturesque village of Alrewas, long ago a centre of basket weaving. Below Alrewas Lock the canal merges with the River Trent for a short distance before the river plunges unnervingly over a large weir. The towpath is carried over a mill stream, the main channel of the river, and a succession of reedy backwaters by an attractive series of metal footbridges somehow reminiscent of the Thames. BW's last ditch enthusiasm for attaching number plates to their structures reached its illogical conclusion with bridges 45a-g. Unfortunately, in their zeal to attach plates to as many static objects as possible, it was reported that a number of anglers had been unwittingly targeted.

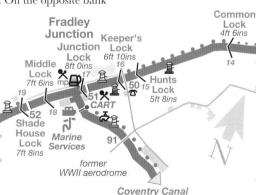

Garden Centre

15

*54

Kings Bromley Wharf

mp

Ravenshaw Wood

Wood End Lock
5ft 2ins

20
53
mp

Fradley Junction

Junction Lock
8ft 0ins

Keeper's Lock
6ft 10ins
16

Middle Lock
7ft 6ins

17

19

51

52
Shade House Lock
7ft 8ins

18

50
15

Hunts Lock
5ft 8ins

CART

Marine Services

91

former WWII aerodrome

Coventry Canal to Fazeley

Common Lock
4ft 6ins

mp

14

pipe

54

A513 to Rugeley

49

49A
Bagnall Lock
5ft 7ins

13
70°

cricket ground

former mill

River Trent

weir !

mp

46 12

Alrewas Lock
5ft 8ins

47

48

Co-op

Alrewas

Alrewas
(csd 1965)

National Arboretum

A38

A513

117

⚠ **Beware the current on the river section between Alrewas and Wychnor locks!**

N

turn to page 34 for details of Fradley Junction and Alrewas and their facilities

33

Fradley Junction
Map 16

Quintessential canal junction, perennially popular with motorists and boaters alike.

Eating & Drinking
THE SWAN - canalside, Fradley Junction. Tel: 01283 790330. *Good Beer Guide* listed former boatmen's pub plays a leading role in the social life of Fradley Junction. Open from 11am daily. DE13 7DN

CANALSIDE CAFE - Tel: 01283 792508. Cafe located in part of the former maintenance yard buildings. Outdoor waterside tables too. DE13 7DN

KINGFISHER CAFE - cafe connected to holiday park. Tel: 01283 790407. DE13 7DN

Shopping
Groceries, gifts and coffees from the Canal Shop.

Connections
TAXIS - Alrewas Taxis. Tel: 01283 790391.

Alrewas
Map 16

A cricket ground and thatched cottages set the tone for this fundamentally pretty village not overly compromised by the grafting on of new housing. Pronounced 'Ol-ree-wuss', the name is derived from the presence of alder trees in the vicinity which were used in basket making. A 'woolly rhino' skeleton was discovered in gravel workings across the A38 in 2002. Experts dated the remains back to the Ice Age and established that it had weighed in the region of one and a half tons. Thankfully its descendants no longer live in the vicinity. Alrewas Mill has been converted into apartments. Within living memory it flourished as a regional manufacturer of animal feeds with a distinctive fleet of delivery lorries. Up until the outbreak of the Second World War its name was painted prominently on the roof. Naturally it had to be painted out, lest enemy aviators employed it to identify their position. Finally, if you're entering the village from Bridge 46 along Post Office Road, keep your eyes peeled

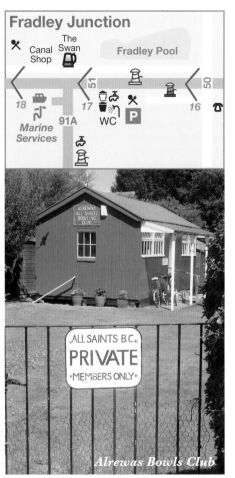

Alrewas Bowls Club

for the unintentionally amusing spelling of 'Coronation Square'.

Eating & Drinking
ALREWAS CANTONESE - Tel: 01283 790027. Chinese takeaway. DE13 7AE

ALREWAS FRYER - Tel: 01283 790432. Excellent fish & chips. Lunch and evenings Mon-Sat. DE13 7AE

THE CROWN - Post Office Road. Tel: 01283 790328. Comfortably refurbished pub/restaurant. DE13 7BS

DELHI DIVAN - Kings Bromley Road (near Bagnall Lock). Tel: 01283 792743. Indian restaurant. DE13 7DB

GEORGE & DRAGON - Main Street. Tel: 01283 791476. *Good Beer Guide* listed Marston's pub offering a good range of food plus accommodation. DE13 7AE

WILLIAM IV - William IV Road (near Bridge 46). Tel: 01283 790206. DE13 7AW

Shopping
The *piece de resistance* here is Peter Coates butcher's shop on Main Street (Tel: 01283 790205 - DE13 7AE) specialising in locally reared meats, boasting a wide choice of game, and also dealing in excellent pies, cheese, flour and vegetables. There is also a pharmacy & post office, and Co-op store with cash machine.

Things to Do
NATIONAL MEMORIAL ARBORETUM - Croxall Road (approximately 1 mile south of Bridge 49A - beware busy roads. (Bus 7E connects Alrewas village centre with the Arboretum on Sundays). Tel: 01283 792333. Developing, not to say moving attraction incorporated in the National Forest as a tribute to those affected by wars. Fifty thousand trees have been planted on a 150 acre site beside the River Tame. Two minute silence, Reveille and Last Post enacted daily at 11am. Shop, and cafe/restaurant. DE13 7AR

Connections
BUSES - Service 7 operates approx hourly Mon-Sat and bi-hourly as 7E on Sundays to/from Burton and Lichfield Tel: 0871 200 2233.

TAXIS - Alrewas Cars. Tel: 01283 790391.

KEEPING company with the Roman's Ryknild Street, the canal traverses the broad, flat valley of the Trent; a landscape of gravel workings and distant villages backed by low-lying hills. Between Alrewas and Wychnor the canal suddenly assumes a quite different character as it negotiates a marshy, almost ethereal stretch of countryside, criss-crossed by drainage channels, or 'sitches', which thread their way through meadowlands to meet the Trent. It is a sudden, yet subtle, scene change. The domesticity of Alrewas village and the cacophony of the A38 are briefly forgotten, as the waterway puts you tantalisingly in touch with a past inhabited by eel-catchers, reed-cutters and sluice-keepers. Watch out for the undertow at Wychnor Lock!

Wychnor was the scene of a tradition, similar to the more famous one at Dunmow in Essex, whereby any man who could swear not to have wished to exchange his wife for another woman, at any time during the first year of his marriage, was entitled to a flitch of bacon from the Lord of the Manor. It may - or may not - surprise you to learn that the flitch was never successfully claimed. Demurely perched above the canal, Wychnor Church

dates back to the thirteenth century although the brick tower is a much later addition. The imposing building across the road at Wychnor Lock was, in more measured days, the Flitch of Bacon coaching inn.

Business parks cluster along the A38 corridor. Central Rivers is a maintenance depot for diesel trains. The massive distribution centre for Argos dominates the landscape unequivocally and is doubtless filled with what Nanci Griffith once described in an introduction to *Love at the Five and Dime* as 'unnecessary plastic objects'. Barton Marina has become a huge success, a honeypot for boaters and land-based visitors alike. The wharf at Barton Turn, presided over by a handsome canal company house, was provided for the villages of Barton and Walton, each a mile or so from the canal on opposite sides of the Trent. When the bridge across the river to Walton was damaged by floods in the 1940s, it was replaced by a 'temporary' Bailey bridge - so temporary that it is still in use.

Tatenhill Lock lies in a deceptively remote setting, and beside the adjoining fishing lagoons are warnings to anglers displayed in Polish. A path runs from Bridge 35 between old gravel workings in the direction of the village of Tatenhill, tucked between folds of the Needwood Hills. The Forest of Needwood was once one of the largest royal hunting grounds; little woodland now remains, although trees are returning with the establishment of the National Forest. Four miles to the north-west lies England's centre of footballing excellence, St George's Park.

for details of facilities at Barton-under-Needwood turn to page 36

Barton-u-Needwood   Map 17

Mellifluously named but much enlarged village with good shopping facilities and several pubs approachable via footpath or B5016. Barton Marina attracts growing numbers of visitors, but the core of the village itself is still worth seeking out, not least the substantial parish church given to the village by its distinguished native, John Taylor, a 16th Century Master of the Rolls.

Eating & Drinking
APPLE TREE - Barton Marina. Tel: 01283 712332. Deli and coffee shop with waterside tables. DE13 8DZ
BARTON TURN - Bridge 38. Tel: 01283 712142. Open daily noon to 11pm. Cosy canalside pub serving Marston's and guest ales. Homely menu. DE13 8EA
NIPA - Barton Marina. Tel: 01283 329303. Part of the Siam Corner group, this stunningly appointed restaurant is open daily for lunch and dinner. DE13 8DZ
RED CARPET - Barton Marina. Tel: 01283 716257. Cinema and cafe bar. DE13 8AS
REGALES - Lichfield Road. Tel: 01283 712345. Indian restaurant, access off towpath opp marina. DE13 8EH
THE WATERFRONT - Barton Marina. Tel: 01283 711500. Hugely popular bar/restaurant with a nice line in real ale and a wide choice of food. Waterside terrace. Live music from 10pm Fri & Sat. DE13 8DZ
There is also a Tea Room at the marina office.

Shopping
BUTCHER BAKER - Barton Marina. Tel: 01283 711002. The name encompasses most of this excellent outlet's activities, but it also offers fresh vegetables, deli items and basic provisions more than a little useful for boaters. Sister shop at Mercia Marina. DE13 8DZ
Barton Marina hosts a range of retail outlets ranging from clothing and furnishing through gifts to shoes. In the village there is a Co-op, post office, pharmacy and cycle shop.

Connections
BUSES - Arriva service 7 connects Barton with Lichfield and 7 & 7A with Burton. Tel: 0871 200 2233.
TAXIS - Ambassador. Tel: 01283 544700.

Branston   Map 18

Once a village, and the unlikely birthplace of a well known relish, now a much-expanded suburb; hardly pretty, but useful for its facilities reached via a pedestrian underpass beneath the A38.

Eating & Drinking
BRIDGE INN - canalside Bridge 34. Tel: 01283 564177. Former boatman's pub serving Marston's beers and Italian food, a curious combination, though not as curious as the purple canal depicted on the inn sign. Pleasant canalside garden. DE14 3EZ

Burton-on-Trent   Map 18

In brewing terms, Burton is an Indian Pale shadow of its zenith, the town's economy revolving just as much around distribution these days as beer: Boots, Waterstones and Holland & Barrett have huge warehouses adjoining the canal and the juggernaut is the favoured means of transport as opposed to the narrowboats or shock-absorbed railway vans of yore. So much traditional brewery infrastructure has 'Gone for a Burton' that former residents, returning after a long absence, would be hard pressed to recognise the place. Burton is at its prettiest in and around the washlands (or 'hays') which border the Trent. Perhaps it was always thus, for that is where the monks chose to erect their long vanished abbey, and where they started brewing beer: liquid history, so to speak.

Eating & Drinking
THE ALBION - Shobnall Road. Tel: 01283 568197. Marston's 'two for one' pub 5 minutes walk north-west of Shobnall Basin past the brewery. DE14 2BE
ALFRED - Derby Street. Tel: 01283 562178. Once the long vanished brewer Truman's 'tap', now part of the Burton Bridge estate. DE14 2LD
THE BREWERY TAP - National Brewery Centre, Horninglow. Tel: 01283 532880. Gastro-pub style food served 11am-11pm Tue-Sat, closes 6pm Mons and open 12pm-6pm Suns. DE14 1NG

BURTON BRIDGE INN - mile south of Horninglow Wharf. Tel: 01283 536596. Worth the lengthy trek to sample the town's doyen micro-brewery. DE14 1SY
CANALSIDE CAFE - Shobnall Marina. Tel: 01283 619590. Open 9am-4pm. DE14 2AU
COOPERS TAVERN - Cross Street. Tel: 01283 532551. Cosy treasure owned now by Joule's. Turn right off Station Street on your way into the town. DE14 1EG
There is easy access from the visitor moorings by pipe bridge 33D (along Third Avenue) to a plethora of eating establishments: a Beefeater, Flaming Grill, McDonald's, Harvester, Toby Carvery and Morrisons supermarket cafe.

Shopping
The town centre is 15-20 minutes walk from the canal, though buses operate from both Horninglow and Shobnall. Market days Thur-Sat. Morrisons supermarket is nearest the canal at Centrum, accessed from pipe bridge 33D. Marston's Brewery Shop lies a tempting 250 yards west of Bridge 33.

Things to Do
NATIONAL BREWERY CENTRE - Horninglow Street (10 mins walk from Horninglow Wharf) Tel: 01283 532880. Open 10am-6pm daily, admission charge. Fascinating displays concerning the history of brewing. Tours include four sample beer tastings. Shire horse and rail and road transport exhibits. DE14 1NG
CLAYMILLS PUMPING STATION - 5 minutes walk from Bridge 29, Map 19. Open Thursday & Saturday 10am-5pm for static viewing, and on special steaming days detectable by a pall of smoke over the surrounding countryside. Tel: 01283 509929. Four beam engines and five boilers in a Grade II listed sewage pumping station dating from 1885. DE13 0DA

Connections
BUSES - local services throughout the Trent Valley and South Derbyshire. Tel: 0871 200 2233.
TRAINS - frequent CrossCountry services to/from Birmingham, Derby, Nottingham etc. Tel: 08457 484950.
TAXIS - Station Taxis. Tel: 01283 532000.

THE famous brewery town of Burton-on-Trent presides over the Trent & Mersey Canal's change of gauge: east of Dallow Lane the locks are widebeam. When the canal opened in 1770, it brought a rapid decline in the use of the River Trent, which had itself been made navigable up to Burton at the beginning of the 18th century. To serve wharves established on the riverbank, however, a branch canal was built from Shobnall to Bond End. When the Birmingham & Derby Junction Railway was opened a drawbridge was provided to carry the line over this Bond End Canal. In 1846 a southbound train plunged into the canal because the bridge had been opened for the passage of a boat in the sadly erroneous belief that no train was due!

Bridge 34 at Branston is a popular mooring point for boaters attracted by the canalside pub and adjoining water park. Between Branston and Shobnall the canal runs at the foot of an escarpment. The half-timbered house on the hill is Sinai Park which belonged to the Benedictine monastery founded in the town in 1004. The main part of the abbey lay beside the river, but Sinai Park was used variously as a hunting lodge, summer house and blood-letting sanatorium.

It is at Shobnall that the canal traveller becomes most aware of Burton-on-Trent's stock in trade. West of the canal stands Marston's high-chimnied brewery, to the east the phalanxed grey silos of Molson Coors Maltings. Visitors are quick to remark upon the aroma of hops in the vicinity, though locals are largely inured to the aromatic tang of the town. A common misapprehension is that Burton derives its excellence in brewing from Trent water. In fact the water used for brewing lies on beds of gypsum rock beneath the town and is pumped to the surface. The predominance of such stone made Burton a centre for the production of alabaster ornaments in the middle ages.

One of the once numerous branch railways, linking the main lines with Burton's breweries and other industries, paralleled the canal on its way through the town. Nowadays known as the Kingfisher Trail, it's used as a public footpath and cycleway. In its heyday, Burton's 'internal' railway system was so dense that there were an astonishing thirty-two level crossings in the town. The railways captured the bulk of beer transport from the canal, but at the end of the 18th century large volumes of ale were being carried along the Trent & Mersey for export via Hull to northern Europe, the Baltic and Russia, and via Liverpool to India and South America. Now, of course, the beer goes out by road, and you will witness Pedigree and Hobgoblin lorries being loaded in the vicinity of Bridge 33C. At Horninglow Wharf, a salt warehouse once spanned the canal, and boats heading east appeared to vanish into a 'tunnel'.

Sinai Park

🚲 54

Branston
Lock
3ft 0ins

33E

D

34

8

Water Park

17

mp

Toby Carvery
Harvester

Flaming
Grill

Beefeater

McD's

Centrum

Morrisons

Marmite

A38

Branston

Branston
(csd 1930)

River Trent

Marston's
Brewery

33C

B

33

Molson
Coors
maltings

industrial
estate

Shobnall
Fields

32B

mp

Shobnall
Marina

Town
Hall

B&Q

Coopers

Town Centre 1/2 mile

National
Brewing
Centre

MI

32A

Dallow
Lane
Lock
3ft 6ins

Nisa

A38

32

Horninglow
Wharf

Burton-on-Trent

Sainsbury's 'Local'

Alfred

54

19

37

EAST of Burton, the Trent & Mersey doesn't exactly flaunt its freshly acquired widebeam status. True, the bridge-holes are more buxom, but it is not until Stenson Lock is reached, that the true gauge of the canal manifests itself. Barge wide vessels traded upwards from Nottingham to Horninglow until the railways took a grip of the trade in beer; thereafter, even narrowboat traffic dwindled. One of the last regular consignments was of cardboard for the manufacture of cigarette papers by Players at Nottingham.

Bridge 31 carries a comparatively new road occupying the trackbed of the North Staffordshire Railway's Burton to Tutbury branchline, haunt of a push & pull shuttle known as "The Jinnie". Nearby is Burton Albion Football Club's 'state of the art' Pirelli Stadium. Tyre making is a lesser-known facet of the brewery town's economy, as is the manufacture of animal feed supplements by Rumenco, a company whose trading name derives from the fact that cows are ruminants and have four 'stomachs'.

Time was when the mill race from Clay Mills marked the boundary between Staffordshire and Derbyshire, now the River Dove is the demarcation. The canal crosses the river upon a low-slung aqueduct of a dozen stone arches designed by Brindley circa 1768 and sketched by J. M. W. Turner (with a horse hauling a boat across it) forty years later. Beloved of Izaak Walton, the River Dove

is virtually at journey's end here, being less than a mile from its lonely confluence with the Trent at Newton Solney; all a far cry from the glories of Dovedale and the Peak District. An adjacent road bridge, reputedly built by the monks of Burton Abbey, compensates for the aqueduct's plain appearance. On sultry summer days, in spite of dangerous whirlpools and official admonitions to the contrary, local youths swim in this reach of the Dove. An imposing Georgian wharf house overlooks Bridge 26 and the site of Egginton's old village wharf. Otherwise the canal is largely featureless as it makes its way through the Trent Valley, as if handcuffed by the portly escorts of a busy dual-carriageway and a main line railway. Southwards, the stiletto-fine spire of Repton church is a notable landmark.

Five redundant cooling towers loom over Willington on a site earmarked for a gas-fired power station. Essentially a commuter village, Willington nevertheless sets its stall out to attract canal visitors. Up until the 1930s, a rail/canal transhipment wharf stood between the milepost and Bridge 23. The Trent & Mersey Canal had been bought out by the North Staffordshire Railway in 1847.

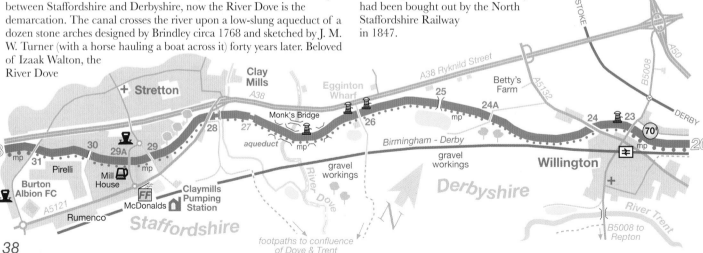

Willington
Map 19

Hardly picturesque, and bedevilled by traffic, but a more than useful watering-hole none the less. The bridge over the Trent dates from 1839, and there was once a cheese factory alongside it. St Michael's diminutive parish church stands modestly nearby. Inside, a plaque commemorates Morgan Maddox Morgan-Owen (1877-1950), Welsh international footballer, much decorated Great War hero, and the Repton schoolmaster reputedly responsible for instigating that public school's adherence to the round ball game as opposed to the oval. Omnibus aficionados will recognise Willington as the original home of the fondly remembered Blue Bus Services, an independent operator whose origins could be traced back to 1922. Two rural routes were faithfully served between Derby and Burton-on-Trent along either side of the Trent Valley. The restricted dimensions of the railway overbridge dictated the use of 'lowbridge' double-deckers. The company's garage at Willington was destroyed by fire in 1976, nineteen vehicles being lost in the inferno.

Eating & Drinking
THE DRAGON - The Green. Tel: 01283 704795. Award-winning and well-appointed pub/restaurant which backs onto the canal. Breakfasts 8-11am daily. Restaurant open from noon to 3pm and 5.30-9pm Mon-Thur and from noon throughout the day Fri-Sun. Good choice of (often local) real ales. DE65 6BP
GREEN MAN - adjacent Bridge 23. Tel: 01283 702377. Cosy, beamy 'local' serving Marston's, guest ales and home-cooked food. DE65 6BQ
KAY'S - The Green. Tel: 01283 703321. Tea room and take-out. DE65 6BP
RISING SUN - The Green. Tel: 01283 702116. DE65 6BP
SUN HALL - Twyford Road. Tel: 01283 703131. Chinese takeaway. DE65 6DG
A fish & chip shop is due to open in 2015.

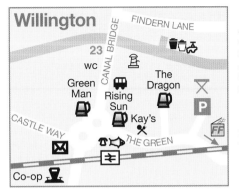

Willington FINDERN LANE

23 CANAL BRIDGE
wc
Green Man
The Dragon
Rising Sun
Kay's
CASTLE WAY
THE GREEN
Co-op
FF
P

Shopping
Co-op store with cash machine (re-sited through the railway bridge), post office, and florist: should you want to say "sorry" for shouting at her at the lock. Betty's Farm on Castle Way (Tel: 0791 718 6393 - DE65 6BW) has a farm shop open daily with butchery Wed-Sat.

Connections
BUSES - V3 'Villager' service runs hourly Mon-Sat (bi-hourly Sun) to/from Derby, Repton and Burton-on-Trent. Tel: 0871 200 2233.
TRAINS - sparse Cross-Country services to/from Derby and Birmingham. Tel: 08457 484950.

Repton
(Map 19)

Pinpointed by the slender spire of St Wystans, Repton is a worthwhile fifteen minute (pavemented) walk (or short bus ride) from the canal across the Trent. The church is of Saxon origin, Repton having been the capital of Mercia in the 9th century until laid waste by marauding Danes. The village is best known for its public school (location of the 1939 film *Goodbye Mr Chips*), its most famous son these days being one Jeremy Clarkson. Several good inns and a farmhouse tea room offer refreshment.

Mercia Marina
Map 20

An impressive cornucopia of boating facilities, eating & drinking establishments and retail outlets in the modern mould. Highlights include: The Boardwalk Bar & Dining (Tel: 01283 702669) and Butcher Baker Farm Shop and Coffee House (Tel: 01283 707325). There is also a tea room and a convenience store. DE65 6DW

Findern
Map 20

Straggling village sliced in half by the A50. Facilities on this side of the trunk road are limited to NADEE at Bridge 21, an Indian restaurant converted from former canalside pub. Tel: 01283 701333. DE65 6AR

Stenson
Map 20

Eating & Drinking
STENSON LOCK COTTAGE - Tel: 0796 669 5914. Popular lockside cafe. Bacon butties! DE73 7HL
THE BUBBLE INN - Tel: 01283 703113. Bar, restaurant and 'boutique' hotel adjoining marina. DE73 7HL

Twyford
Map 20

Since the chain ferry was damaged by floodwater in 1963 - and heinously not repaired - Twyford has led a sequestered existence at the end of a cul-de-sac, visited by few save for lovers and church crawlers.

Barrow-on-Trent
Map 20

Peaceful village on a bend of the Trent. Pinfold on the lane to the church: for straying cattle not parishioners.

Eating & Drinking
THE RAGLEY BOAT STOP - Deepdale Lane (between bridges 17 & 18, offside customer moorings). Tel: 01332 703919. One of the King Henry's Taverns group of well-appointed East Midlands pubs. DE73 7FY
BROOKFIELD - village centre. Tel: 01332 700128. Thriving 'not for profit' community pub. DE73 7HG

20 TRENT & MERSEY CANAL Stenson 4mls/11k/2hrs

IT was at Findern that 'the worst storm either of us had ever experienced, raging without pause for over three hours' overtook Tom and Angela Rolt aboard *Cressy* in 1939, as described in L. T. C. Rolt's seminal book *Narrow Boat*. A few days later an even greater storm erupted as Britain declared war on Germany. Quite what the reactionary Rolts would have made of the canal's latest cynosure, the massive Mercia Marina, is open to conjecture, but there's no doubting its impact on this part of the Trent & Mersey and the local economy.

When the railway was built, track ballast was sourced locally, by the simple expedient of digging it out of the ground. The holes thus formed filled with water and became amenities. An old signal box was purloined to act as a pavilion, and a boat provided from which to sit and fish or simply to sit and wonder. In its working days the power station was allowed to stuff these charming ponds with waste ash. But one between the railway and the canal has been revived and equipped with a pond-dipping platform,

making it a nice spot to have a picnic whilst pondering on the certain truth that today's cutting-edge technology is tomorrow's leisure opportunity. Talking of technology, Toyota's huge car plant can be seen on the skyline beyond Mercia Marina.

Between Stenson and Swarkestone the canal slinks furtively through fields given largely over to vegetable growing. The feeling that one is a long way from anywhere is misleading. Derby lies just over the rim of the northern horizon. Even closer is the busy A50 trunk road, which serves as a link between the M1 and M6 motorways. But then canals have a knack of conjuring a stimulating sense of isolation in the most unpromising of circumstances. Near Bridge 16, a moving little memorial commemorates the tragic death of a teenage girl in 1978.

The railway which parallels the canal most of the way between Stenson to Sawley lost its regular passenger services thirty years before Beeching reared his hideous head, though from time to time diverted passenger trains still use it at the weekends. Normally, only goods trains rattle over its tracks now, and the wistfully named wayside station of Castle Donington & Shardlow is as distant a memory as working boats on the canal.

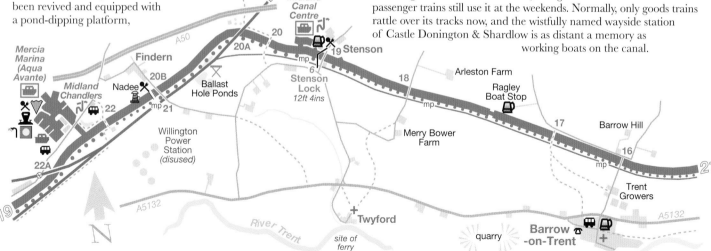

turn back to page 39 for details of facilities at Mercia Marina, Stenson Marina etc

NEVER more than half a mile away from the Trent, and often closer, the canal travels through mellow countryside, much of which is given over to market-gardening. Evidence of occupation by the Beaker People sixteen hundred years before the birth of Christ suggests that man's influence on Swarkestone goes a long way back. Swarkestone Bridge is of relatively modern origin, dating back only to the 12th century. It is generally regarded as the longest stone-built bridge in Britain. In 1347 the scale of tolls quoted charges of a ha'penny for a cask of sturgeons. In 1745 this was the furthest south that Bonnie Prince Charlie's army got in their attempt to capture the throne of England. Just twenty-five years later the Trent & Mersey was being dug, and soon afterwards Swarkestone

became the site of a junction with the Derby Canal, including a branch down to the river which only survived until around 1800.

The Derby Canal, overlooked by nationalisation in 1947, was acrimoniously abandoned in 1964, though trade had ceased twenty years earlier. The company who owned the canal were well aware that more money could be made from property deals than from running a public waterway. The old junction house remains intact, used, like the one at Huddlesford on the Coventry Canal, by a local boat club. The Derby Canal's towpath has been resurfaced as part of National Cycle Route 6 and there are ambitious plans to restore at least part of the canal (which linked with the Erewash Canal at Sandiacre) to navigable standard.

By Weston Cliffs the canal glides through tumbling woodland. While construction of the canal was proceeding eastwards, a wharf was erected here for the transfer of goods from barge to riverboat. Later it was used for the transhipment of gypsum bound from Aston to King's Mills, whereupon, after being ground, the resultant plaster was despatched back up the canal for consignment via Swarkestone and the Derby Canal to a building merchant in Derby. In these days of the ubiquitous lorry, the labour-intensiveness of previous eras of transport is astonishing.

continued overleaf:

course of Derby Canal
A50

A514 to Derby

S.B.C. &6

Swarkestone Stop 14 13A

15 5 13

20 mp Cuttle Bridge

Swarkestone Lock
10ft 11ins

course of Derby & Ashby Railway

A50

Swarkestone Nursery

Crewe & Harpur
A5132

The Stand

Swarkestone
Hall

12 mp

&6

River Trent

Swarkestone Bridge

Sailing Club

Stanton -by-Bridge
A514 to Swadlincote

70'

site of military railway depot
Tarasivka

11A 11

course of Derby & Ashby Railway
viaduct

Weston Cliffs

viaduct

site of bridging school

&6

Derby Cycle Route
(Melbourne 1 mile)

10
mp

former wharf

9

Weston-on-Trent
Cooper's Arms

Weston
(csd 1930)

8
4
mp

Weston Lock
10ft 11ins

Derbyshire

Weston Grange

mp

7

7A

River Trent

site of ferry

site of lock

King's Mills

Leics.

22

continued from previous page:

During the Second World War this dreamy riparian landscape was rudely awakened by the construction of an army camp at Weston Cliffs. It was built to house the army's railway engineers who operated the Melbourne and Ashby line as a military railway during the Second World War. The army camp also provided accommodation for soldiers attached to a Bridging School opened across the river at King's Newton. As part of their training they built a now vanished suspension bridge across the river to facilitate access between the camp and the school. The enigmatic remnants of a steam crane used by the bridge-makers remains by the handsome cast-iron railway viaduct which now carries Cycle Route 6 across the Trent near Bridge 11. The trackbed of that line has been imaginatively resurfaced to create a traffic-free link between Derby and the handsome old market town of Melbourne.

Hardly had the railway engineers marched away, before the camp was commandeered to house Ukrainian refugees. Several hundred arrived here to escape oppression in their homeland in 1944. Weston Rectory, visible on its low hilltop to the north of the canal, was used as a home for the centre's elderly residents, whilst parts of the camp were used by Ukrainian youth groups. A number of Ukrainian children were accommodated here following the Chernobyl nuclear disaster. The camp is known as Tarasivka and includes a tiny wooden chapel and a memorial to those who gave their lives for freedom in the Ukraine.

The lane from Bridge 8, by Weston Lock, provides easy access to Weston village in one direction. In the other it offers a peaceful walk down to the site of an old lock opposite King's Mills, a popular bathing spot until demolition of a weir in 1957 rendered such activities dangerous. Rummage in the undergrowth and you may discern the remains of the old lock. In the past there was a ferry here too, providing access to the mills on the Leicestershire bank of the Trent - sadly it is no more.

Swarkestone Map 21

There is a good view from the canal of The Stand, an intriguing 17th century pavilion surmounted by a picturesque pair of ogee domes which is thought to have been used as a grandstand for viewing bear-baiting or jousting, though more probably simply bowls. There was once a great mansion here belonging to the Harpurs, who decamped to Calke.

The Landmark Trust - a company of angels who make it their business to reinvigorate unwanted architectural treasures and make them available for holiday lets - has restored the pavilion as accommodation for just two occupants, who must be tolerant enough to accept a bathroom approached by way of the roof terrace! The Rolling Stones used The Stand for a photo-shoot in 1968.

Eating & Drinking
CREWE & HARPUR - Tel: 01332 700641. A well-appointed Marston's '2 for 1'country inn and restaurant with accommodation. DE73 7JA B&B also available at Swarkestone Lock House - Tel: 01332 702406.

Swarkestone Stop

Connections
BUSES - service 61 runs hourly, daily to/from Derby and Swadlincote. In the latter direction it calls at Melbourne, an engaging small town. Tel: 0871 200 2233.

Weston on Trent Map 21

Potentially confusing, this is the *second* Weston-on-Trent that the Trent & Mersey encounters on its travels - the other one being south of Stone.

Eating & Drinking
COOPERS ARMS - Weston Hall. Tel: 01332 690002. Charming lakeside establishment housed in handsome 17th Century mansion used by Cromwell as a temporary barracks. During the First World War an escaped German prisoner hid here briefly before eventually making his way back to his homeland. Bar/carvery/restaurant food. Real ales from Derby Brewing Co. DE72 2BJ

Connections
BUSES - service 73 runs hourly Mon-Sat to/from Derby. Tel: 0871 200 2233.

NAVIGATION from the Trent to the Mersey must have seemed like a proclamation for travel from the earth to the moon, but this was how the fledgling canal company advertised its purpose back in 1780. The words adorn the largest warehouse at Shardlow, the company's 'inland port', once known waggishly as "Rural Rotterdam". And Shardlow, unlike its counterpart Preston Brook, at the other end of the Trent & Mersey, has been fortunate enough to retain the greater part of its historic infrastructure. Pride of place goes to the handsome Clock Warehouse, now a popular pub, alongside Shardlow Lock. Like many of Shardlow's warehouses, it owes its survival to F. E. Stevens, a local animal feeds merchant, whose occupation of this, and several other canalside buildings, secured a use for them in the century which passed between the cessation of the local canal trade and a new era of refurbishment for leisure and commercial use. Look carefully, and you'll come across evidence of F. E. Stevens' use of Shardlow in faded signwriting on many a wall. Indeed, Shardlow deserves to be lingered over and not rushed through, whatever their current use - commercial or domestic - the old warehouses are somehow still redolent of their original role, and it isn't difficult to airbrush out the imperfections of the present and picture the port in its animated heyday.

Although it is Shardlow which appears on the distinctive Trent & Mersey mileposts, the actual junction with the Trent Navigation is at Derwent Mouth, approximately one and a half miles east of the village. It's a short journey, as easily accomplished on foot as afloat, and the Derwent Valley Heritage Way commences its 55 mile journey to Ladybower Reservoir from beside the lock. The much shorter walk to Sawley is possible once again following provision of a spanking new footbridge across the Trent just upstream of Derwent Mouth.

Downstream the Trent, forming the boundary between Derbyshire and Leicestershire, sweeps haughtily towards Nottingham, an eye-opener for boaters passing through Derwent Mouth Lock and away from the cosy world of the canals. You pass beneath a pipeline which brings water supplies down from the Peak District to slake the thirst of Leicester folk, and you pass beneath the M1 motorway on which the traffic often seems to be moving more slowly than you.

As the Trent tumbles over a weir and passes beneath Harrington Bridge, a canalised cut brings you to Sawley Bridge Marina and its extensive facilities. East of here Sawley Locks are duplicated, automated and usually manned in the summer months. Further coverage will be found in the *East Midlands Canal Companion*.

for details of facilities at Shardlow and Sawley turn to page 44

Shardlow

Map 30

Attractive Georgian village much quieter now that the A50 has siphoned off the heavy traffic that used to plague its main street on what was once designated the A6; the trunk road from London to Carlisle. Shardlow Hall was built in 1684 by Leonard Forsbrook from profits made on the river trade. The maltings prominent by Cavendish Bridge house the Shardlow Brewing Company, 'Narrowboat' being one of their most popular brews. There was once an orphanage in the village, foundlings being given the surname Shardlow.

Eating & Drinking

CLOCK WAREHOUSE - adjacent lock. Tel: 01332 792844. Popular refurbishment of Shardlow's most iconic warehouse. Marston's ales, a wide menu, and archive photographs on the walls. DE72 2HL

SMITHY'S MARINA BAR - Shardlow Marina. Tel: 01332 799797. Bar and restaurant. DE72 2GL

THE NAVIGATION - London Road. Tel: 01332 792918. DE72 2HJ

THE NEW INN - The Wharf. Tel: 01332 793330. Pole position on the canal. Pedigree, Bombardier and up to three guest ales. Wide choice of food. Open from 10am daily. DE72 2HG

THE MALT SHOVEL - The Wharf. Tel: 01332 799763. Erected 1799 and once owned by the local brewery Zachary Smith & Co which stood on the opposite side of the canal. DE72 2HG

DOG & DUCK - London Road. Tel: 01332 792224. Cosy Marston's pub housed in building dating back to 15th Century. DE72 2GR

SHAKESPEARE INN - London Road. Tel: 01332 792728. Former coaching inn. DE72 2GP

OLD CROWN - Cavendish Bridge. Tel: 01332 792392. *Good Beer Guide* regular across the county boundary in Leicestershire. DE72 2HL

TANDOORI NIGHTS - London Road. Tel: 01332 853383. Indian restaurant. DE72 2GP

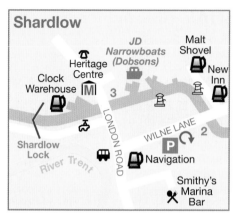

GOLDEN DRAGON - Cavendish Bridge. Tel: 01332 799158. Chinese restaurant & takeaway. DE72 2HN

Shopping

Small post office stores a bit of a hike along the old A6, one mile west of the canal.

Things to Do

HERITAGE CENTRE - Canalside, London Road. Tel: 01332 814104. Open Easter to October, Sat & Sun (plus Fri Jul-Sep) 12am to 5pm. At first you think you've just parted with seventy-five pence to peruse a gallimaufry of junk. But this charming little museum - housed in Shardlow's oldest canal warehouse - rapidly weaves its magic on you, and were it not for the fact that half a dozen visitors constitutes a crowd and that others are waiting patiently outside to get in, you find yourself beguiled into staying for hours, not least because the enthusiastic volunteers who devote their time and love into running it have so much knowledge to impart. The story of the rise and fall of this inland port and the village's other activities are delightfully portrayed. Exhibits range from old boatbuilding tools to a mock-up narrowboat cabin, but we would have gladly paid that 75p just to see the sepia photograph of the Clock Warehouse with a horse and cart in front of it where now the car park sadly lies. DE72 2GA.

Connections

BUSES - Skylink services (provided by the Loughborough-based independent, Kinch) run half-hourly, daily to Loughborough and Leicester (via East Midlands Airport) and Derby - Tel: 0871 200 2233.

TAXIS - Shardlow Cars. Tel: 01332 793173.

Sawley

Map 30

Suburban sprawl to the north, but handsome church (with an unusually wide nave) and core of original village near the river.

Eating & Drinking

THE MARINA CAFE - Sawley Marina. Tel: 0115 946 0300. Breakfasts from 8am. NG10 3AE

PLANK & LEGGIT - adjacent Sawley Marina. Tel: 0115 972 1515. All-day family orientated pub with 'Wacky Warehouse' play barn. Two meals for a tenner Mondays to Fridays. NG10 3AD

HARRINGTON ARMS - Tamworth Road (opposite church on B6540). Tel: 0115 973 2614. This whitewashed former coaching inn is now a Hardy's House with cosy interior and large garden. NG10 3AU

THE WHITE HOUSE RESTAURANT - Tamworth Road. Tel: 0115 972 1261. Stylish contemporary restaurant. NG10 3AU

Connections

BUSES - 20 minute interval Skylink service from stop outside marina to/from Nottingham (via Long Eaton railhead) and Loughborough (via East Midlands Airport). Tel: 0871 200 2233.

TRAINS - local railhead at nearby Long Eaton from which there are frequent services to/from Derby, Birmingham, Nottingham, Leicester and London St Pancras. Tel: 08457 484950.

TAXIS - Erewash Taxis. Tel: 0115 946 4440.

Gailey Roundhouse

Staffs & Worcs Canal

23 STAFFS & WORCS CANAL Acton Trussell 4mls/11k/2hrs

LARGELY unmolested, the canal slips quietly through the outskirts of Stafford. The county town stood an aloof mile to the west of the Staffs & Worcs Canal which, in true Brindley fashion, followed the easy contours of the Penk Valley. Plans to construct a branch were dropped in favour of a simple lock down into the Sow, the river being dredged and realigned to take boats as far as a terminal basin at Green Bridge in the centre of Stafford. The navigation was opened in 1816 and in use until the end of the First World War. A footpath follows the riverbank into the town, but it is difficult to envisage how seventy foot narrowboats ever got up there. A group known as Stafford Riverway Link has been formed to promote restoration of this long lost route as a boost to the county town's economy.

Baswich church once stood as isolated on its hillside as Acton Trussell's does still, but now it is surrounded by a housing development, though those with an interest in ecclesiastical architecture can easily reach it from Bridge 100. Note the spelling of the village's name with a 'k' on the bridgeplate. There was a substantial wharf by Radford Bridge, but its site is now somewhat less interestingly occupied by a car showroom following demolition of the original warehouses in the Philistine seventies.

Stafford Boat Club - with their impressive club house and welcome to visiting boaters - occupy a former brickworks arm near Hazelstrine

Bridge. Most of the works's output was despatched by canal. Bridge 97 has disappeared completely, there being not even any tell-tale narrowing in the canal's channel where it once must have stood.

Radford Meadows form part of the River Penk's floodplain and are now administered by the Staffordshire Wildlife Trust as a nature reserve. Public access is restricted to special events, but the towpath offers fine views (and interpretive boards) of what is nowadays quite a rare environment. Radford's signature species is the rare Black Poplar tree. Snipe, which in the past would have bred here in significant numbers, are also being encouraged to return.

The lock-keeper's cottage at Deptmore had been, throughout most of the life of the *Canal Companions*, the home of a reclusive character, whose only means of contact with the outside world had been by means of a motorised pontoon which was kept in an off-side lay-by at the tail of the lock. Now, following a period of abandonment, a track has been forged through the fields and the house is being renovated.

Acton Trussell - which you'd expect with such a name to be a picture book English village - fails to live up to expectations with its banal modern architecture. The solitary building on the towpath side used to be a boatman's pub. Present day boaters, however, slake their thirst in the old moated house by Bridge 92, now well-established as a bar, restaurant and hotel set in charming grounds. It is said that Brindley actually used the old house's moat for a few yards when building the canal: anything to save a few bob.

46

Stafford Map 23

One of England's lesser-known county towns, Stafford has always seemed too self-effacing for its own good; though there are signs that in recent years it has begun to wake up to its tourist potential. Unfortunately for canal folk, the centre lies over a mile from Radford Bridge. But there are frequent buses, and those with time at their disposal will find Stafford a rewarding place to visit. First stop should be the Ancient High House in Greengate Street - the main thoroughfare. Dating from 1595, it's thought to be the largest timber-framed town house remaining in England. Inside there's a heritage exhibition tracing Stafford's history since 913 when Ethelfleda, daughter of Alfred the Great, fortified the settlement against marauding Danish invaders. King Charles I stayed at High House in 1642, and in later years Izaak Walton visited relatives who owned it. An alleyway beguiles you off Greengate Street to discover the town's large parish church of St Mary, much restored by Gilbert Scott in the 1840s and containing a bust of Izaak Walton. Another delightful church worth visiting is St Chad's on Greengate Street. Elsewhere, some impressive buildings reflect the town's administrative status, lending it, in some instances, an almost metropolitan air.

Eating & Drinking
RADFORD BANK - canalside Bridge 98. Tel: 01785 242825. Crown Carvery. ST17 4PG
THE SOUP KITCHEN - Church Lane. Tel: 01785 254775. Open 9am-5pm Mon-Sat. Quaint, sprawling eatery (enhanced by attentive waitresses) serving coffees, lunches and teas. Rooftop garden. ST16 2AW

Shopping
Good shopping centre featuring all the well known 'high street' names plus many attractive individual shops tucked away down twisting side streets. Large Asda and Tesco supermarkets. Indoor market (Earl Street) Tue, Thur, Fri & Sat. Farmers' Market on the second Saturday in the month. Co-op

'Convenience Store' accessible from Bridge 100 at Baswich if you're just passing through.

Things to Do
TOURIST INFORMATION - Gatehouse Theatre, Market Street. Tel: 01785 619619. ST16 2LT
ANCIENT HIGH HOUSE - Greengate Street. Tel: 01785 619131. Local history and gifts. ST16 2JA
SHIRE HALL GALLERY - Market Square. Tel: 01785 278345. Exhibitions, crafts and coffee bar housed in an imposing late Georgian building overlooking the Market Square. ST16 2LD
STAFFORD CASTLE - Tel: 01785 257698. Well preserved Norman castle on town's western outskirts. ST16 1DJ

Connections
BUSES - services throughout the district. No.s 1,2,3,74 & 825 connect Radford (Bridge 98) at frequent intervals with the town centre. Tel: 0871 200 2233.
TAXIS - AJ's Tel: 01785 252255.
TRAINS - Important railhead with wide variety of services. Tel: 08457 484950. Useful links with Penkridge and Rugeley for clued-up towpath walkers.

Acton Trussell Map 23

THE MOAT HOUSE - canalside Bridge 92. Tel: 01785 712217. Four star hotel in former moated farmhouse: restaurant and bars, verdant grounds. ST17 0RG

Penkridge Map 24

A not uninteresting little town, and a good place to break your journey on the northern section of the Staffs & Worcs. Five minutes walk from the wharf will take you to the narrow main street, a pleasant spot to shop and saunter. At its foot - but mind the traffic on the A449 - stands St Michael's, an impressive church of sandstone, and formerly a collegiate church, considered second only to a cathedral in ecclesiastical status. The interior contains some splendid tombs and memorials to the Littleton family.

Eating & Drinking
CROSS KEYS - canalside Bridge 84. Tel: 01785 712826. A once isolated pub, described by Rolt in *Narrow Boat*, but now surrounded by a housing estate, though that doesn't diminish its popularity with boaters and motorists alike. ST19 5HJ
THE BOAT - Bridge 86. Tel: 01785 715170. Canalside pub. Real ales, home-made food and football on TV. ST19 5DT
FLAMES - Mill Street. Tel: 01785 712955. Contemporary Eastern cuisine housed in one of Penkridge's most historic buildings. ST19 5AY
More pubs and fast food in the town centre.

Shopping
Convenience shops by bridges 84 and 86. The town centre, with its Co-op (inc post office) and other retailers, is 5 minutes walk from the canal. Down by the river, the outdoor market operates on Wednesdays, Saturdays and Bank Holiday Mondays.

Connections
BUSES - to Cannock, Wolverhampton and Stafford. Tel: 0871 200 2233.
TRAINS - hourly London Midland services to Wolverhampton and Stafford. Tel: 08457 484950.

Coven Map 26

Coven's village centre is less than ten minutes walk from Bridge 71, but do take care crossing the A449!

Eating & Drinking
FOX & ANCHOR - canalside north of Bridge 71. Tel: 01902 798786. Flourishing Vintage Inns establishment offering a wide choice of food and drink. WV9 5BX
Fish & chip shop in the village centre.

Shopping
Co-op foodstore, butcher (on the road in) baker, pharmacy, and post office. Secondhand bookshop adjoining the butcher, open Thur-Sat 11.30am - 4pm. Tel: 01902 791833.

24 STAFFS & WORCS CANAL Penkridge 4mls/7lks/3hrs

AS the canal ascends to (or descends from) its summit level, the locks come thick and fast. The motorway retreats, only to be replaced by the housing estates which cling-wrap the essentially agreeable little town of Penkridge. Yet, a mile on either side, the countryside is characterised by rolling farmland lifting to the bulwark of Cannock Chase.

The towpath between bridges 90 and 86 is hi-jacked by the "Staffordshire Way" which seems forever to be bumping into canals and appropriating towpaths in the course of its 92 mile journey from Mow Cop to Kinver Edge. Its route has come down off The Chase and crossed Teddesley Park. Teddesley Hall was the seat of Sir Edward Littleton, one of the chief promoters of the Staffordshire & Worcestershire Canal. Indeed, the family remained involved with the canal company until its nationalisation in 1947. The hall itself was demolished by the army in the mid Fifties (having been used as a prison camp for German officers during the Second World War) but the estate farm remains, hidden from the canal by some woodland known as Wellington Belt in commemoration of a visit to the hall by the Iron Duke. Bridge 89 once had ornate balustrades commensurate with its importance as the gateway to the hall, but, irresponsibly and unforgivably, these have been infilled by ugly brickwork.

Rather sadly, the Teddesley Boat Company has ceased offering boats for hire. One by one these family firms, who were at the forefront of the hiring boom which hit the canals in the nineteen-seventies, are ceasing to operate or being taken over, and the canal scene is somehow poorer for their passing.

Many boaters pause to take on water at Penkridge Wharf, but there is usually room to moor up for a visit to the town. The Littletons had fingers in many pies, not least the local colliery, which at one time employed over a thousand men. A huge basin, now covered by the motorway, was constructed to enable boats to be loaded with coal from a raised pier by gravity. The chief traffic flow of Littleton coal by canal in later years was down

to Stourport Power Station. The mine closed in 1993. Rodbaston Lock had a keeper until the motorway was built. A special bridge was built over the new road to maintain access to his lockside cottage, but the noise of the ensuing traffic was so bad as to cause him to leave and find new accommodation, the cottage subsequently being demolished. West of the canal between Otherton and Rodbaston lies a college of agriculture.

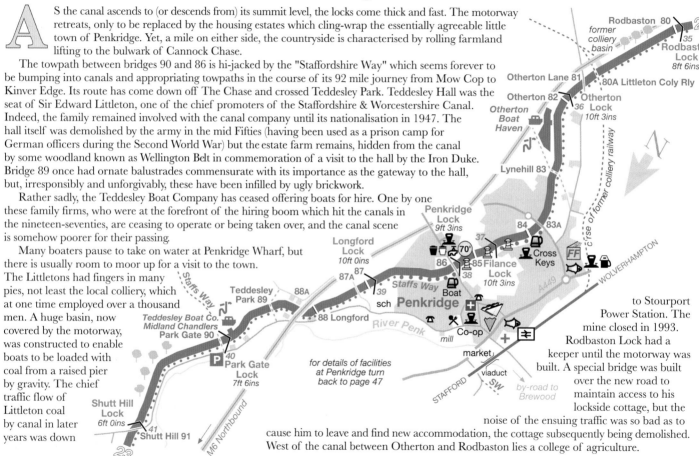

for details of facilities at Penkridge turn back to page 47

25 STAFFS & WORCS CANAL Gailey & Hatherton 3mls/3lks/2hrs

CALF HEATH is a strangely isolated tract of country, pancake flat and crossed by a grid of sullen little roads, with here and there a huddle of houses, gathered reassuringly together like something out of Van Gogh's early potato field paintings. The canal all but boxes the compass of this gravel pit-riddled landscape, so that The Chase with its communications tower and the chemical works with its phalanx of flaring chimneys, appear to move about you, teasing you into geographic insecurity, like a game of Blind Man's Buff.

The Staffs & Worcs Canal's summit - from Gailey to Compton - lies at more or less 340 feet above sea level. If you've climbed up from Penkridge and beyond it's a relief to be done with locks for the time being. Industry lines the canal at Four Ashes. A former tar works here was once served by Thomas Clayton boats.

The last load of Cannock coal came off the Hatherton Branch in 1949 and it was abandoned a couple of years later. However, the illusion of a junction remains, because the bottom lock (of what was once a flight of eight in three miles) is still used to provide access to moorings. The Lichfield and Hatherton Canals Restoration Trust is actively seeking restoration of the branch with the intention of linking it with the northern waters of the BCN at Norton Canes, and there is little doubt that its opening would prove a great fillip to the under-boated northern extremities of the BCN.

Watling Street crosses the canal at Gailey. The most significant feature here is the 'round house', originally a toll clerk's office but now a splendid canal shop run by mother and daughter team, Eileen and Karen Lester; the former a keen Wolves supporter, the latter favouring Villa. There is something spell-binding about cylindrical buildings - Martello towers, windmills, lighthouses; even Birmingham's Bull Ring Rotunda - and Gailey roundhouse, in its lock-side setting, has a particular charm which begs to be captured on camera.

Summary of Facilities
A short walk westwards along the A5 will take you (past a nursery with tea room) to Gailey roundabout and a number of potential attractions: a small general store; a pottery housed in a former church; a large Marston's pub called the Spread Eagle; and Dobbies Garden World. Arriva bus 76 runs hourly to Penkridge and Wolverhampton.

THE world is divided - though not perhaps equally - into those of who think of The Laches as Plato's Socratic dialogue on the nature of courage, and those who think of it as a bridge on the Staffordshire & Worcestershire Canal. Knowing full well which category it falls into, the canal imperviously exchanges the loneliness of Calf and Coven heaths for the industrial and suburban outskirts of Wolverhampton; the M54 to Telford forming an obvious, though not intentional, boundary.

At Cross Green a former boatman's pub called "The Anchor" has transmogrified into the "Fox & Anchor", a popular restaurant bar, and many boaters choose to moor here overnight. As it passes beneath the M54 the canal crosses the county boundary between Staffordshire and the West Midlands, one of the new counties which had its origins in the local government changes of 1974. Many people still mourn the old counties. It must have been galling, for instance, to have lived in Lincolnshire all one's life and wake up one morning in the absurdity that was

South Humberside. West Midlands was possibly the dullest of all the new names, and sounds as though it must have been the compromise of a committee. *Black Country* would have been a far more appropriate and resonant title.

The most significant feature of this length is "Pendeford Rockin", the old boatmen's name for a shallow, but tellingly narrow cutting hewn by Brindley's navvies through a solid belt of sandstone which breaks through the clay strata at this point. The cutting, half a mile or so long, restricts the channel to such a degree that you begin to wonder if you have lost concentration and taken a wrong turn. There are, however, one or two passing places - as on a single lane road - where oncoming boats can be successfully negotiated without losing one's temper. As the canal moves towards Autherley Junction it skirts the perimeter of a large school, screened from the waterway by an intimidating line of Lombardy poplars which have the look of teachers sternly trying to keep order at Morning Assembly.

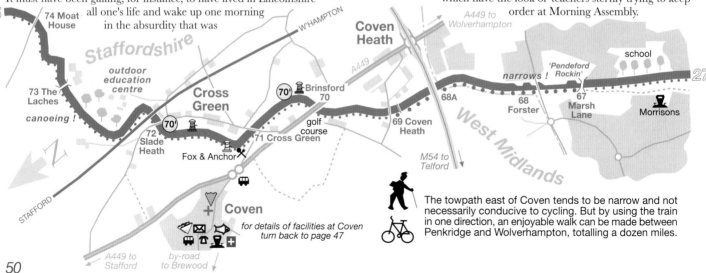

The towpath east of Coven tends to be narrow and not necessarily conducive to cycling. But by using the train in one direction, an enjoyable walk can be made between Penkridge and Wolverhampton, totalling a dozen miles.

for details of facilities at Coven turn back to page 47

Shropshire Union Canal

Woodseaves Cutting

27 SHROPSHIRE UNION CANAL   Autherley Junction 3mls/11k/1hr

DESPITE the proximity of Wolverhampton, Autherley, like many canal junctions, is self-contained. It is not pretty in a conventional sense, being bordered by housing estates, sewage plants and public open spaces. In typically pithy fashion, the old boatmen called it 'Cut End', for the obvious reason that the Shropshire Union Canal began and, more pertinently, ended here. Once there was all the paraphernalia of a meeting of waterways: toll office, stables, workshops, employees cottages, and a dominant, sweeping roving bridge carrying the Staffs & Worcs towpath over the entrance to the Shropshire Union. A stop lock - just six inches deep - protected the two companies' precious water supplies. Much of this infrastructure survives, enjoying a new lease of life in the leisure age as a hire base and boatyard.

A massive sewage plant provides the canal with much of its water; suitably treated of course, or perhaps this explains the Shropshire Union's apparent impatience to get on with its journey to the north-west. Whatever the motivation, Autherley is soon forgotten as the canal crosses the boundary between the West Midlands and Staffordshire and leaves Wolverhampton's urban fringes behind. At Bridge 2 - if you can find your way between the houses - you can go and view a 17th century dovecote, incongruous in its 21st century setting.

The land east of the canal was once occupied by an aerodrome, whilst the works by Bridge 4 was formerly an aircraft factory, turning out, amongst other designs, the 'Defiant' fighter plane. A fascinating little museum was being developed here by enthusiastic members of the Boulton Paul Aircraft Heritage Project. Unfortunately, however, the site was sold in 2013 and all the exhibits - a replica aircraft, a range of memorabilia, and reconstructions of the company's boardroom and a crash site in the Peak District - have had to be stored at nearby RAF Cosford pending establishment of a new museum in an appropriate setting elsewhere.

An 'invisible' aqueduct carries the canal over the little River Penk before the waterway goes through a series of contortions which incur a sequence of narrowings and widenings before resuming its usual width beyond Bridge 7. Temporarily, the M54 impinges, but otherwise the landscape is serene and unruffled, setting the scene for the forty mile journey to Nantwich through some unexpectedly remote countryside. Characteristic cast iron mileposts display the distances between Autherley and Nantwich with Norbury Junction thrown in for good measure.

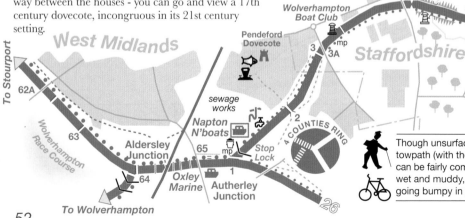

Though unsurfaced for the majority of its length, the Shropshire Union towpath (with the notable exception of Woodseaves Cutting - Map 33) can be fairly comfortably walked, though footwear can quickly become wet and muddy, especially in the winter months. Cyclists will find the going bumpy in places, and should anticipate punctures.

THE Shropshire Union slices through the Staffordshire countryside in cuttings and upon embankments typical of the bold, 19th century designs of Thomas Telford, who engineered this route between Autherley and Nantwich, originally known as the Birmingham & Liverpool Junction Canal.

Travelling northwards you rapidly become attuned to the unique atmosphere of this canal. Far from becoming monotonous, its purposeful, loping stride across the landscape is strangely exhilarating, perhaps due to the recurring contrast of shadowy cuttings and panorama providing embankments, known as 'rockings' and 'valleys' respectively to past generations of boatmen.

years) shot a marauding panther.

North of Brewood, the canal crosses the old Roman Road of Watling Street on a sturdy, yet elegant aqueduct of iron, brick and stone construction: it occurs to us that some time has elapsed since it last benefitted from a coat of paint. Nearby Belvide Reservoir is another of the main sources of water supply for the Shropshire Union Canal. It is also, under the auspices of the West Midland Bird Club, a magnet for ornithologists. Broom Hall, east of Bridge 16, was the home of William Carlos who hid King Charles II in the oak tree at nearby Boscobel after the Battle of Worcester in 1651.

for details of facilities at Brewood turn to page 54

There are notable structures either side of Brewood. To the south the curvaceously ornate, balustraded Avenue Bridge (No 10) carries the carriageway to Chillington Hall. The advent of the canals heralded many similar attempts at ornamentation and disguise, where powerful landowners would only condescend to permit a waterway to cross their parklands if suitable steps were taken to adorn the otherwise purely functional architecture of the new trade route. Chillington itself lies about a mile and a half to the west in grounds landscaped by Capability Brown. En route you encounter Giffard's Cross, where in the sixteenth century one of the Giffards (who have inhabited the estate for over eight hundred

Boatbuilding and maintenance is undertaken at Stretton Wharf, beyond which the canal is once more engulfed by one of its trademark cuttings. For a while activity on the towpath is augmented by walkers on the Staffordshire Way which seems to encounter a good many canals on its wanderings between Kinver and Mow Cop. Devotees of the *Canal Companions* may care to learn that this very map was - way back in 1981 - the prototype from which all the maps in the series evolved. In its first guise it was hand drawn on cardboard, with a perspex flap for the second colour, and its lettering cut out and stuck on with gum; all a far cry from the Apple Mac which shoulders the work now.

Brewood Map 28

Probably because it is so close to the county boundary, Brewood feels more like Shropshire; there being a 'West Country' richness about it that doesn't pertain, for example, to nearby Penkridge. And there really is a timelessness about 'Brood' which seduces you into spending longer here than you might have planned. Winding lanes of gracious houses lead to the old market place, enhancing one corner of which is 'Speedwell Castle', a Gothic fantasy erected in the 18th century on the winnings of a racehorse named Speedwell. The tall-spired parish church is notable for its Giffard family tombs. In the churchyard lies the grave of Hugh Rose, a Scots engineer who came here to build the canal. The Roman Catholic church, by Bridge 14, is the work of no less a Victorian architect than Augustus Welby Northmore Pugin.

Eating & Drinking

BRIDGE INN - Bridge 14. Tel: 01902 903966. Much extended former boatmans' pub. Marston's & guest ales. Home cooked food. Open from noon. ST19 9BD
THE CURRY INN - Church Street. Tel: 01902 850989. Eat in or take-away Indian. Opens 5pm. ST19 9BT
LION HOTEL - Market Place. Tel: 01902 850123. Stylishly decorated inn offering accommodation, bar and fine dining, opens 9am daily. ST19 9BS
THE MESS - Market Place. Tel: 01902 851694. Charming daytime cafe and evening restaurant. ST19 9BS
POWELLS TEA ROOM - Market Place. Tel: 01902 851921. ST19 9BJ
THE SWAN HOTEL - Market Place. Tel: 01902 850330. Cosy *Good Beer Guide* listed pub with skittles. ST19 9BS

Shopping

Spar (with cash machine), Co-op (inc post office) and branch of Lloyds Bank (9.30am-2.30pm, Mon, Tue, Thur & Fri only). Coopers foodstore is excellent, as is the Village Bakery for filled baps. Butchers W. Maiden & Son (Tel: 01902 850346 - ST19 9DX) are easily missed at the far end of Stafford Street, but shouldn't be, for they

Speedwell Castle

are a long-established family concern. You can see pies being made on the premises and take away that Black Country delicacy, 'gray paes' or Staffordshire oatcakes. Nice old-fashioned hardware store in Market Place.

Things to Do

CHILLINGTON HALL - about a mile and a half west of Bridge 10. Tel: 01902 850236. The imposing 18th century house (incorporating earlier structures) and its grounds are open to the general public for special events on selected dates. WV8 1RE

Connections

BUSES - the Green Bus Co, whose venerable buses had so endeared themselves to us for over thirty years, have sadly ceased to operate, but the void has been filled by the Select Bus Co. whose services 877/8 operate hourly Mon-Sat to/from Wolverhampton with some continuing via Wheaton Aston to Penkridge and Stafford. Tel: 0871 200 2233.
TAXIS - Codsall Cars. Tel: 01902 840000.

Wheaton Aston Map 29

Once purely a farming community, Wheaton Aston has been overwhelmed by modern housing and continues to grow. No picture postcard village, then, but at least it appears to be thriving, defying the trend towards rural decline.

Eating & Drinking

HARTLEY ARMS - Bridge 19. Tel: 01785 840232. Canalside pub offering a range of food. ST19 9NF
COACH & HORSES - High Street. Tel: 01785 841048. Throwback Banks's local. Cafe open for breakfasts from 8.30am Tue-Sun. ST19 9NP
MOMTAJ SPICE - High Street. Tel: 01785 841381. Bangladeshi restaurant and take-away housed above the Coach & Horses. ST19 9NP

Shopping

There's a small convenience store and post office on the way into the village if you're in a rush, but the village's most enterprising shop is undoubtedly the Spar opposite the church. It's open daily 7am-10pm and, along with all the other to be expected requisites, does a nice line in filled baguettes, and ready-to-eat pies and pasties: mind you, you have to push past half the village in there gossiping to get to the counter! Turner's canalside garage stocks Calor gas, diesel and boating accessories. Free range eggs from Bridge Farm.

Connections

BUSES - Select 877/8 as Brewood. Tel: 0871 200 2233.

WHEATON ASTON Lock is strangely solitary - the only one in twenty-five miles of canal; a telling measure of Telford's advanced engineering techniques. For about a mile the canal penetrates the deciduous heart of Lapley Wood, and there's another typical Shroppie cutting by Little Onn, but elsewhere the embankments offer wide views eastwards towards Cannock Chase; and beyond, perhaps, to a tell-tale plume of steam from Rugeley's power station.

Sadly (though perhaps understandably) access is by permit only (Tel: 01743 282000) but those who do venture with authority into this unchanged landscape can encounter such rarities as the Horsetail Weevil and Snake's Head Fritillary, the latter at its most northerly discovered location.

One of the canal's lengthy embankments carries it across a sequence of culverts which provide access between neighbouring fields. It also spans a brook which flows eastwards into the River Penk, registering the fact that this is the watershed between the Trent and the Severn. The ghost of a Roman Road bisects the canal at the southern end of Rye Hill Cutting.

Abandoned wartime aerodromes inevitably have their ghosts, and in decay accumulate a patina of lore and legend, hard perhaps to equate with the often mundane use to which they were put after closure. Wheaton Aston was opened in 1941 and became one of the RAF's largest training units, operating a squadron of 'Oxfords'. There were at least two canal dramas:

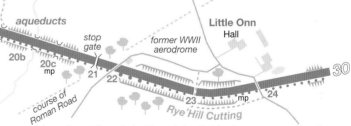

How astonishingly remote and unpeopled the landscape seems. The West Midlands conurbation is less than a dozen miles to the south, yet moor for the night between Wheaton Aston and Little Onn, and you'll have only the occasional eerie hoot of a hunting owl, or the distant silent wash of headlights on a country lane, for company. Something of this sense of isolation must explain the survival of Mottey Meadows, alluvial flood meadowlands, unploughed for centuries, whose name apparently derives from the French word for peat - *motteux*.

once an American 'Thunderbolt' crash-landed in the waterway. Another well remembered wartime incident occurred at the lock when a narrowboat, carrying an unsheeted cargo of shining aluminium on a moonlit night, was attacked by a German aircraft which unleashed a bomb that exploded less than a hundred yards from the chamber. After the war the aerodrome's inhospitable huts were used for some twenty years as a transit depot for displaced persons, primarily Poles. Subsequently the site became a pig farm. So much for the hospitality of the British!

55

Avenue Bridge, Chillington

Brewood

Woodseaves

Shropshire Union Canal

Shelmore Embankment

The Boat Inn, Gnosall

Tyrley Cutting

AUTHERLEY JUNCTION. 24 MILES.

NANTWICH 15 MILES.

NORBURY JUNCTION. 8¾ MILES.

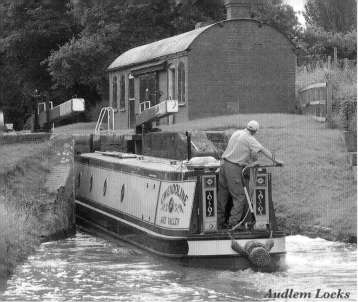

Audlem Locks

Nantwich Aqueduct

Audlem Locks

The Middlewich Branch

57

PERSISTING in its self-absorbed hike across the empty landscapes of west Staffordshire, The Shroppie even attempts to shun the little town of Gnosall, the name of which recalls to mind that old comic song by Flanders & Swann about The Gnu. In this case, you don't say Ger-no-sall, you say No--zull.

Deep shadowy sandstone cuttings, spanned by lichened grey stone bridges of simple balance and unaffected dignity, lead to the eighty-one unlined yards of Cowley Tunnel; the only one on the Shropshire Union. Once a dizzy jungle of trees darkened the approaches so much that you were never quite sure where the tunnel began and the cutting ended,

On a clear day the embankments north of Gnosall reveal that famous Shropshire landmark, The Wrekin, 15 miles to the south-west; a slumbering hunchback of a summit, 1335ft high. A. E. Housman celebrated it in *A Shropshire Lad* - 'his forest fleece the Wrekin heaves' - and Salopians raise their glasses in a toast to: "All friends around the Wrekin".

Now in use as a public footpath (the Stafford Newport Greenway), the dismantled railway line which crossed the canal at Gnosall once usefully connected Stafford with Shrewsbury until a certain Doctor made his presence felt. Historically it was unusual in that it was actually built by the Shropshire Union Canal Company, apparently hedging their bets on the transport mode of the future. When, in 1846, they leased themselves to the London & North Western Railway, few shareholders would have backed the canal to outlast the railway as it has done.

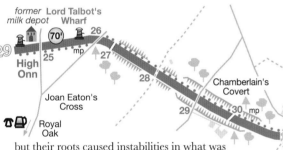

but their roots caused instabilities in what was already a brittle rock strata and they were felled in 1985. Nature - *naturally* - is already well advanced with the work of healing the scars. These cuttings are apt to play aural and olfactory tricks on your senses. The blended aromas of bacon and diesel hang enticingly in the air and voices carry much further than you'd think: so be inclined to temper your remarks concerning the odd looking couple on that last boat you passed.

The buildings of two wharves remain intact at High Onn. One - now converted into a most desirable home - belonged to Cadbury's, the other to a local landowner, suggesting that there was once a degree of agricultural traffic on the canal.

The Way For The Millennium is a forty mile long distance footpath connecting two extremities of Staffordshire, Newport to the west and Burton-on-Trent to the east. As far as Stafford it utilises the trackbed of the old railway, thereafter it follows the towpaths of the Staffs & Worcs and Trent & Mersey canals for much of the remainder of its course.

Church Eaton   Map 30

Shopless village made remote by the huge tract of apparently empty countryside which characterises west Staffordshire. There's some Kempe glass in the church.

Eating & Drinking

ROYAL OAK - High Street (approx 15 mins walk east of Bridge 25). Tel: 01785 823078. *Good Beer Guide* listed, whitewashed, community-owned pub offering bar and restaurant food. Banks's, Marston's and local micro-brewery beers. ST20 0AJ

Gnosall   Map 30

Gnosall Heath thrived with the coming of the canal and the railway not long afterwards, Gnosall stood back and watched with alarm, the onset of Progress. Two pubs slaked the thirst of passing boatmen, a steam powered flour mill took advantage of the new transport mode, and a non-conformist chapel kept a sense of proportion amidst all the excitement. Nowadays the pubs pander to pleasure boaters and passing motorists and the flour mill and chapel have become private residences. Half a mile east of the canal, Gnosall slumbers on its hilltop, the substantial parish church of St Lawrence being its most notable landmark.

Eating & Drinking

THE BOAT - Bridge 34. Tel: 01785 822208. Marston's/Banks's pub with attractive curved wall abutting the bridge. Food available and pleasant garden by the water's edge. ST20 0DA

THE NAVIGATION - Bridge 35. Tel: 01785 822327. Nice garden with good children's playground. ST20 0BN.

THE GASTRONOMY SHOP - High Street. Tel: 01785 824616. Charming cafe/deli. ST20 0EX

Fish & chips on A518 open daily (except Sundays), both sessions. Tel: 01785 822806. Chinese takeaway in Gnosall - Tel: 01785 824388.

Shopping

General store (with cash point) and butcher by Bridge 34. Co-op in Gnosall itself, together with post office, off-licence, florist, grocer and deli (see E&D).

Connections

BUSES - Arriva service 481 half-hourly Mon-Sat, hourly Sun, to/from Stafford and Newport. Tel: 0871 200 2233.

Norbury Junction   Map 31

An atmospheric canal community, and although the suffix is misleading nowadays, Norbury remains a busy canal centre where the Canal & River Trust have a maintenance yard. Norbury Wharf operate a trip boat and offer laundry facilities.

Eating & Drinking

OLD WHARF TEA ROOMS - canalside Bridge 38. All-day, all year licensed cafe; sizeable portions of homely cooking. Tel: 01785 284292. B&B and s/c accommodation also available. ST20 0PN

JUNCTION INN - canalside Bridge 38. Tel: 01785 284288. Busy pub popular with boaters and motorists alike. Garden with children's play area. Bar and restaurant meals. ST20 0PN

ANCHOR INN - canalside Bridge 42. Tel: 01785 284569. Famously unspoilt boatman's pub which has been in the same family for generations. Devizes-brewed Wadworth 6X from the jug. Sandwiches served to order. *Good Beer Guide* fixture. ST20 0NB.

HABERDASHERS ARMS - Knighton (half a mile east of Bridge 45 on Map 32). Tel: 01785 280650. Oil lit, quarry-tiled throwback. Open from 12.30pm daily ex Wed & Thur when it opens from 7pm. ST20 0QH

Shopping

Boatyard shop: provisions, off-licence, gifts, chandlery and a wide choice of canal books.

The Anchor, High Offley

31 SHROPSHIRE UNION CANAL Norbury Junction 4mls/0lks/1hr

ALL trees disguise the immensity of Shelmore embankment and unfortunately curtail what would otherwise be panoramic views. It was six years in the making and, in its way, was as glorious an engineering feat as any of Telford's more visibly imposing aqueducts. A veritable army of navvies and horses was employed on it. Spoil from the big cuttings at nearby Gnosall and Grub Street was brought by wagon for its construction. To Telford's dismay - conscious as he was that the bank need not have been tackled at all, had Lord Anson of Norbury Park sanctioned the preferred course through Shelmore Wood - the earthworks slipped time after time and, as the rest of the canal was finished, Shelmore stubbornly

Norbury is no longer a junction, though the name lives on, and a roving bridge spanning an arm which leads to a dock at least sustains the illusion of another canal heading off into the unknown. The Newport Branch was abandoned by the LMS Railway in 1944, yet how nice it would be now to lock down its 'Seventeen Steps' and head across the marshy emptiness of Shropshire's Weald Moors to Shrewsbury, encountering Telford's early cast iron aqueduct at Longdon-on-Tern: in many respects a miniature prototype for Pontcysyllte.

Staffordshire's Grub Street is not synonymous with the lower echelons of the literary trade ... though we often feel we have inhabited them for long enough ourselves. No, this Grub Street is known in canal circles as the location of another of the Shroppie's trademark cuttings. For over a mile the canal is wrapped in a thick coat of vegetation, again, like Shelmore, hiding the sheer size of the eighty foot deep cutting, whose most unusual feature is the double-arched bridge which carries the A519 across the canal. The tiny telegraph pole is a survivor from the line which once marched beside the Shroppie for much of its length. Appropriately, canals are again being used as lines of communication with the burying of optical fibres beneath selected lengths of towpath. It is to be hoped that this hi-tech activity meets with the

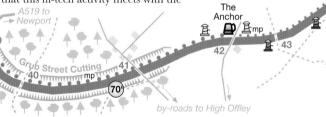

refused to hold. With Telford's health failing, an up and coming engineer called William Cubitt - who was to go on and make a name for himself as a railway builder - deputised. In March 1834 Telford paid his last visit to the canal, and Cubitt accompanied him on a conducted tour. Frail and deaf, the great engineer regarded the embankment which was the cause of so much delay and extra expense. One can picture the younger man confidently reassuring his elderly companion, but a few weeks after Telford's visit the bank slipped for the umpteenth time, and by the time Telford died, on 2nd September, his last canal remained uncompleted. Not until the following January was Shelmore Bank considered solid enough for the canal to be put in water and for the first boat to gingerly proceed across.

approval of the black, monkey-like creature reputed to have haunted Bridge 39 ever since a boatman was killed here in the 19th century. Grub Street Cutting has had its towpath upgraded: thankfully, it is no longer necessary to equip yourself with a pair of fisherman's waders to negotiate it. High Offley's church sits prettily on its hillside.

CROSSING the border between Staffordshire and Shropshire, the canal continues to traverse an uncluttered countryside almost entirely given over to agriculture. A new crop conspicuous in neighbouring fields is elephant grass. It can come as a surprise to find so remote a landscape in the 'crowded' middle of England. One is tempted to categorise the area as 'lost' but for the obvious truth that it has never been 'found' in the first place.

Blithely we pleasure boaters sail across embankments and through cuttings with no more thought for their construction than if we were driving down the M6. But imagine the impact of Telford's brash new canal on the surrounding early nineteenth century landscape. Put yourself in the position of Sir Richard Whitworth's tenant farmer at Batchacre Park. Up until 1830 dawn rose across the open pasturelands throwing light through his east-facing windows. A year later his view of the rising sun was cut off forever by an embankment twice the height of the farmhouse. No wonder the landowners of this rural corner of Staffordshire had their misgivings, and the canal company paid dearly in compensation for the land they acquired. A series of leaks in the vicinity of Shebdon brought about closure of the canal in 2009, but thankfully soil-mixing techniques have now consolidated the bank.

West of the canal, there are good views of The Wrekin, with the Clee and Breidden hills prominent on the far horizon. You wouldn't expect to encounter a factory in the midst of otherwise empty countryside, but you do! It was opened by Cadbury, the chocolate manufacturers, in 1911 as a centre for processing milk collected from the dairy farming hinterland of the Shropshire Union Canal. Canal transport was used exclusively to bring countless churns gathered from numerous wharves along the canal; from simple wooden stages at the foot of fields, to the sophistication of Cadbury's own plant at High Onn. Cadbury owned a distinctive fleet of narrowboats, being one of the first operators to experiment with motorised craft. Cocoa and sugar crumb were also brought by boat to Knighton and blended with milk to make raw chocolate, itself returned to Bournville, again by boat, to be transformed into the finished delicacy. The last boatman to trade to Knighton was Charlie Atkins senior; eponymously nicknamed 'Chocolate Charlie'. He carried the final cargo from Knighton to Bournville in 1961, but some fine examples of historic craft are often to be seen moored here. These days the works trades under the name of Knighton Foods and produces dry powdered ingredients for drinks, desserts and baking products.

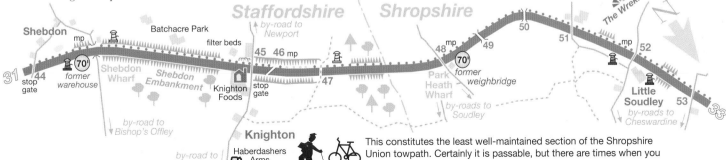

This constitutes the least well-maintained section of the Shropshire Union towpath. Certainly it is passable, but there are times when you just wish the budget would run to a bit more tender loving care.

THE Shroppie flirts with the county boundary. The landscape, however, is impervious to the machinations of local government, remaining aloof and typically inscrutable: a tall, dark, silent canal, this Shropshire Union.

Woodseaves is another prodigious cutting: almost a hundred feet deep in places. Verdure is overpowering. Everything is tinged green; even the milepost at Bridge 57. We were reminded of the boy under the waterfall in *The Box of Delights*. Duckweed thrives in the towpath's plentiful puddles. The canal narrows and, in places, is cut through solid rock. These cuttings proved just as troublesome to Telford and his contractors as did the embankments. In its raw, newly completed state, it must have resembled the canal at Corinth. There were frequent avalanches during construction, and to this day brittle lumps of sandstone are inclined to dislodge themselves and tumble into the canal; reason enough for a 2mph speed limit for boats to be imposed.

There is little chance that towpath walkers can reach this giddy speed, and there ought to be a certificate awarded those who brave the cutting; a certificate, that is, attesting to their lunacy. Alright, you will get through, but you will look like you've been dragged through a hedge backwards by the time you reach the other end. A feature of Woodseaves is its pair of high bridges, spanning the canal-like portals to the mysterious chasms of another world.

At Tyrley (pronounced 'Turley') a flight of five locks - the last to be faced southbound for seventeen miles - carries the canal down into, or up out of, Market Drayton. The lower chambers are located in a shadowy sandstone cutting across which branches intertwine to form a tunnel of trees. Damp, and rarely touched by sunlight, all manner of mosses and ferns flourish in this conducive environment. After dusk bats leave their tree bole roosts to hunt for insects, acrobatically twisting and turning over the luminous pounds between the locks. Fishing rights are under the auspices of Palethorpes Angling Society. We cheerily asked one angler if he'd caught anything: 'Not a sausage,' came the lugubrious reply.

Tyrley Wharf was a point of discharge and collection for the local estate at Peatswood; Cadburys also used to collect milk from here and take it by boat to their works at Knighton. The buildings date from 1841 and were erected in a graceful Tudor style by the local landowner. Nowadays, its commercial significance a thing of the dim and distant past, it would be difficult to imagine a more picturesque location, though those who remember Tyrley in the Eighties still miss the craft shop and home-baking outlet which briefly enlivened the scene here.

Cheswardine
Map 33

Cheswardine lies a country mile to the east - say 25 minutes on foot - of the canal and can be accessed from bridges 52-55. High Street ascends to an imposing parish church much rebuilt by a Victorian architect by the name of Pearson - so it must be good.

Eating & Drinking

THE WHARF TAVERN by Bridge 55 is a popular port of call throughout the boating season and features a spacious canalside garden. The pub opens lunchtimes and evenings daily and there are also self-catering and caravanning facilities. Tel: 01630 661226 - TF9 2LP.

RED LION - High Street. Tel: 01630 661234. A brew pub which prides itself in what it doesn't do: food, jukebox, piped music, fruit machines, television and pool. The landlord used to be Tyrley's lock-keeper back in the Eighties and is very knowledgeable about the Birmingham & Liverpool Junction Canal. *Not open weekday lunchtimes.* TF9 2RS

FOX & HOUNDS - High Street. Tel: 01630 661244. To have one good pub left in an out of the way village smacks of good fortune. To have *two* borders on the miraculous. This one's a Joule's house, so the beer (see opposite) doesn't have far to come. Open Mon evenings, Tue-Fri lunch & evening, Sat & Sun from noon. Food served lunch and evening Tue-Sun. TF9 2RS

Shopping

Delightful community shop adjoining Fox & Hounds. Open Mon-Fri 7.30am-10am and 3pm-5pm; Sat & Sun 9am-11am.

Tyrley
Map 33

Up a leafy lane, ten minutes west of Tyrley Wharf (past Tyrley's reticent little redbrick church) you'll come upon THE FOUR ALLS which offers breakfast, bar and restaurant meals and also accommodation Tel: 01630 652995 - TF9 2AG

Market Drayton
Map 34

The conspicuous Second World War pillbox guarding Bridge 62 is not, despite first impressions, still in situ as a deterrent to visitors. Absentmindedly self-styled as 'The Home of Gingerbread', Drayton is best visited on a Wednesday when the ancient market is in full swing and country folk gather to seek out a bargain and a gossip. This is the town's real heritage, along with its half-timbered houses which mostly date from the aftermath of a fire that swept through the place in 1651. Drayton's most famous son was Robert Clive, best remembered here for scaling the sturdy tower of St Mary's and for blackmailing local shopkeepers - ideal escapades in preparation for a career in diplomacy and military leadership. He established British rule in the Sub Continent and became known as 'Clive of India'. Betjeman and Piper's Shell Guide of 1951 recalls that the district was once terrorised by a murderous gang known as 'The Bravoes of Market Drayton'. On Saturday nights, as the pubs empty, it's easy to believe they are still at large. To the west of the town lie the large premises of Muller - 'the UK's most loved dairy product brand' - whilst on the northern fringe is Drayton's Livestock Market, a flourishing centre for agricultural buying and selling; at times excitable bidding can be heard, borne on the wind as far out as the towpath.

Eating & Drinking

THE TALBOT - adjacent Bridge 62. Tel: 01630 654989. A handsome, red brick Georgian inn just east of the canal. Open lunch and evenings ex Mon. TF9 1HW

RED LION - Great Hales Street. Tel: 01630 652602. Brewery tap for revitalised Joule's. Open from 11am daily. Comfortably furnished, good food, and great to have Joule's (see Map 10) back again! TF9 1JP

ORUNA CUISINE - Shropshire Street. Tel: 01630 658121. TF9 3DA

THE HIPPODROME - Queen Street. Tel: 01630 650820. Wetherspoons in former cinema. TF9 1PS

THE BUTTERCROSS - town centre tea room. Tel: 01630 656510. Coffees & teas, oatcakes & omelettes. TF9 1PF

AMBROSIA DE L'ORIENT - Cheshire Street. Chinese restaurant. Tel: 01630 658382. TF9 1PD

Shopping

It can't be easy for small market towns to compete these days, let alone small independent shops. Yet Market Drayton tries hard and looks its best on a Wednesday, market day. Drayton Deli is a good food shop beside the handsome Buttercross. Branches of all the main banks and a post office, whilst Morrisons, Lidl and Asda supermarkets will cater adequately for most boaters' requirements. 'Busy Dawn' advertises a local collection and delivery laundry service - Tel: 01630 652525.

Things to Do

TOURIST INFORMATION - Cheshire Street. Tel: 01630 653114. TF9 1PH

MUSEUM - Shropshire Street. Tel: 01630 654300. Open Tue, Wed, Fri & Sat mornings from April to October. Admission free. Local history nostalgically displayed in an old shop. TF9 3DA

Connections

BUSES - service 64 operates hourly Mon-Sat to/from Shrewsbury. Service 164 operates at similar frequencies to/from Hanley (Stoke-on-Trent) via Newcastle-under-Lyme. Tel: 0871 200 2233.

TAXIS - First Call Taxis. Tel: 01630 653200.

Adderley
Map 34

Scattered village forgetful of the fact that it once boasted a railway station. The isolated church largely dates from 1800 and is under the care of the Churches Conservation Trust. Lovely ironwork tracery on clear glass windows and a mounting block. Alongside Lock 1 on the Adderley Flight stands Adderley Wharf Farm Shop run by a young couple called Simon and Alison. Free range eggs, home made cakes, lamb, pork and bacon are on sale. Tel: 07710 312747. TF9 3TN

MARKET DRAYTON was the largest, in fact the *only*, town encountered by the old Birmingham & Liverpool Junction Canal on its route from Autherley to Nantwich. Naturally, a sizeable wharf was provided for dealing with local cargoes; though the canal's monopoly on local trade lasted only thirty years before the railway reached the town. It is sometimes difficult, in these days of the ubiquitous juggernaut, to appreciate the importance of the canal wharf and the railway goods yard to the past prosperity of small towns like 'Drayton. They must have been the hub of local life, few businesses would have been able to carry out their trade without regular recourse to the wharfinger and the stationmaster. From the opening of the canal until the First World War no commodity, apart from local agricultural produce, could have arrived at Market Drayton, or been dispatched, without the involvement of these important gentlemen. On the canal a large basin and a sizeable warehouse and adjoining cornmill remind us of this lost significance.

Pleasant 48 hour moorings, bordered by school playing fields, stretch south from Bridge 62 to the imposing aqueduct over the lane to Peatswood - Map 33. Steps lead down to the road below, which crosses the little River Tern nearby and forms the most romantic - but not perhaps the most convenient - approach to the town centre.

The canal makes a quick getaway north of 'Drayton. By Bridge 65, H. Orwell & Son have added boatyard facilities to their traditional business as coal merchants. Note the substantial stone abutments where the North Staffordshire Railway once crossed the canal. The line opened in 1870 and closed in 1956. Passenger services to Stoke, sixteen miles to the east, were fairly sparse, but the railway threw off several profitable mineral branches.

Betton Cutting is not among 'The Shroppie's' most dramatic, but it is reputed to be haunted by a shrieking spectre, and working boatmen would avoid lingering here in the old days. Indeed, it could be said that this whole canal has something of a fey quality about it, a blurring of the homespun and outlandish which is liable to send shivers down susceptible spines.

The five locks of the Adderley flight limber you up for (or warm you down after) the fifteen of Audlem. In 1980 they ran to a resident lock-keeper - who went by the delightfully bucolic name of Frank Butter - and were so beautifully maintained and manicured that they won first prize in the National Lock & Bridge Competition. A privet hedge beside the third lock down indicates the site of a demolished lock-keeper's cottage - one of many to have disappeared from the canal system over the years - whilst a bench commemorates canal stalwart Ike Argent.

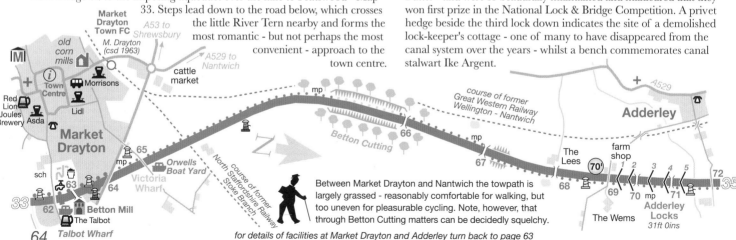

Between Market Drayton and Nantwich the towpath is largely grassed - reasonably comfortable for walking, but too uneven for pleasurable cycling. Note, however, that through Betton Cutting matters can be decidedly squelchy.

for details of facilities at Market Drayton and Adderley turn back to page 63

35 SHROPSHIRE UNION CANAL Audlem 4mls/15lks/3hrs

FIFTEEN locks, running through a cutting of larch and Scots pine, take the canal across the Shropshire/Cheshire border. The locks - trademark 'Shroppie' in their grey paint - are well-maintained and a pleasure to operate, but they can get busy and at such times patience and courtesy have their rewards. To paraphrase some old advice: be nice to people when you're working up lock flights, because you might meet the same people coming down! Enthusiasts of an historical bent may care to know that as built by Telford, the locks on the Birmingham & Liverpool Junction featured mitred gates at the top of each chamber

mill was built during the First World War by H. Kingsley Burton, hence the name. It produced animal feeds, boats brought in raw materials and took away sacks of feed. Old photographs depict a covered gantry which spanned the roadway and jutted out over the canal to facilitate loading and unloading. The mill ceased working in the nineteen-sixties and was converted into a canal shop in the seventies by the late John Stothert, much of its internal fittings and machinery being retained. In recent years Audlem has established itself as the venue of an increasingly popular working boat gathering on the last weekend in July.

Shadowing the Shropshire Union - which belonged to the

Swanbach

Coxbank

A525 to Whitchurch

Audlem (csd 1963)

A529

OverWater Marina Cheshire Cat

Peckforton Hills

crse. of Wellington - Nantwich Rly

Adderley (csd 1963)

Pool House

74

mp

1

2

75

Kinsell Farm

3 76 4 5 6 77 7 8 9 10 11 12 78

mp

Audlem Locks 93ft 0ins

13 14 15 70' aqueduct

79 Moss Hall

mp

Shroppie Fly

Audlem Mill

Bridge Inn

80

Weaver Way mp

36

Hankelow Mill

34 73

Shropshire

Cheshire

River Weaver

(81)

Audlem
for details of facilities at Audlem turn to page 66

A525 to Newcastle

A529 to Nantwich

as well as the tail. This arrangement, however, was shortlived, and the more conventional single gates at the top were installed during the 1840s. One or two of the lock chambers have retained their keeper's cottages, others have lost them, though at Lock 7 you can still smell the scents of garden flowers. A lady sells cakes at the top lock, whilst vegetables and fruit are often available from an honesty box by Lock 9.

The barrel-roofed building by Lock 10 was used by stonemasons, blacksmiths and carpenters engaged in maintaining the flight. Towards the foot of the flight - known to old boatmen as the Audlem "Thick" - you pass Audlem Wharf, one of the prettiest ports of call on the Shropshire Union, with a former warehouse restored as a popular pub and the adjacent lofty Kingbur Mill converted into a superb craft shop. The

London & North Western Railway by the time the railway age was in full swing - the rival Great Western company's Wellington to Nantwich and Crewe route was a useful means of competition. The crane which adorns the wharf outside the Shroppie Fly pub belonged at the railway station before it was resited. Audlem station closed in 1963, but not before it had been immortalised by Flanders & Swann in their melancholy elegy to the Beeching axe, *Slow Train*. Goods predominated, notably a nightly vegetable train carrying the produce of the Vale of Evesham to Manchester's markets. The line continued to be used for another four years, not least by the Pines Express *continued overleaf:*

continued from page 65:

in its twilight days after being diverted away from its traditional route which included the fabled Somerset & Dorset Railway.

Passing a well preserved stable block - home to Pete and Jane Marshall of the Day-Star Theatre - the canal, wide with concrete banking but deceptively shallow, bounds across the strippling River Weaver on a high embankment. One of the crazier notions of the Ministry of War Transport during WWII was to make the Weaver navigable by 100 ton barges to

this point, beyond which a lift would carry them up to the level of the Shropshire Union, upgraded sufficiently for them to travel as far south as Wolverhampton. OverWater is one of the new breed of 'farmland' marinas. A waterbus service links the marina with Audlem on selected days. Bridge 80 retains its early British Waterways era blue and yellow number plate, immediately to the south, a drainage paddle is embossed 'SUC Ellesmere 1928'; minor artefacts of enduring value.

Audlem Map 35

Audlem has grown in confidence and commerce in the years we've known it. Even motorists deign to stop here now, attracted by increasingly sophisticated shopping opportunities. Yet the village seems comfortable with its burgeoning popularity, and appears capable of assimilating visitors without descending into vulgarity. Highpoints include the ancient buttermarket and parish church in photogenic juxtaposition.

Eating & Drinking

THE BRIDGE - canalside Bridge 78. Tel: 01270 812928. Marston's, food daily 12pm-8pm. Nice etched windows pertaining to Marston & Thompson ... who remembers Thompson now? CW3 0DX

THE SHROPPIE FLY - canalside Lock 13. Tel: 01270 812379. Food served daily from noon. CW3 0DX

THE LORD COMBERMERE - The Square. Tel: 01270 812277. *GBG* listed village centre pub. CW3 0AQ

VILLAGE CHIPPY - Cheshire Street. Fish & chips. Tel: 01270 811777. CW3 0AH

OLD PRIESTS HOUSE - The Square. Tel: 01270 811749. All day breakfasts, coffees, teas and light lunches. *Closed Tuesdays.* CW3 0AA

JA's - Cheshire Street. Tel: 01270 811118. Coffee shop; sandwiches & soups. CW3 0AH

AUDLEM KEBAB HOUSE - Tel: 01270 812226. Shropshire Street. Kebabs, burgers, chickens. CW3 0AE

Shopping

Shopping here is a pleasure rather than a stressful chore. Co-op, butcher, pharmacy, post office,

Audlem Wharf

deli/bakery, newsagent/gifts, wine, beer & spirits outlet and bicycle shop. Cash machine at the Co-op. Laundry facilities at Overwater Marina adjacent Bridge 80.

Things to Do

AUDLEM MILL CANAL SHOP - Tel: 01270 811059. Christine and Peter Silvester operate one of the best canal shops on the system and are mines of local information to boot. As well as a wide range of gifts and crafts (not to mention Snugbury's ice cream) the mill stocks an unrivalled range of canal books also available online at *www.canalbookshop.co.uk*. Additional emphasis now on needlework and crafts for which courses are offered. *www.audlemmill.co.uk* CW3 0DX

SECRET BUNKER - Hack Green, Map 36. Tel: 01270 629219. Open 10.30-5.30 daily during summer season plus weekends in winter. Admission charge. Refreshments. "Experience a real four minute warning, view original TV broadcasts to be transmitted in event of a nuclear strike. Authentic equipment in its original macabre setting brings home the power of nuclear weapons and the government's state of readiness. Displays of material from behind the Iron Curtain. "Not just for mum and dad but children too. Soviet Spy Mouse Trail". CW5 8BL

Connections

BUSES - GHA Coaches service 73 to/from Nantwich approx hourly and Whitchurch four times per day Mon-Sat. On Wednesdays service 75 provides a 'one-off' link with Market Drayton worthy of consideration by towpath walkers. Tel: 0871 200 2233.

G RUB Street, *Hack* Green: is the Shroppie scoring literary points? Itinerant canal writers apart, there are two isolated locks and the remnants of a stable at Hack Green, recalling the practice of frequent changing of horses on the 'fly' boats which travelled day and night with urgent, perishable cargoes, the sort of canal age equivalent of a lorry pull-in now. Mow Cop becomes visible on the eastern horizon, a sobering realisation of how little distance you've travelled if you're doing the Four Counties Ring.

This is the Cheshire Plain and dairy farming has long been a vital part of the area's economy - though for how much longer one might wonder, given the precarious state of agriculture in the 21st century. Making a profit from milk is notoriously difficult these days, no wonder farmers are being encouraged to replace cows with canal boats as demonstrated by a growing number of new marinas in the area.

When we first explored this canal in the early Eighties we were blissfully unaware of Hack Green's nuclear bunker, a Second World War radar station secretly designated to play a role as a Regional Government Headquarters in the event of a nuclear war. Deemed redundant at the end of the Cold War, it has somewhat bizarrely become a tourist attraction.

Adroitly changing the subject, let us recall how trade survived on this canal until the 1960s; which must be some sort of testimony to the viability of canal carrying. Perhaps in the final analysis attitudes rather than economics prevailed. One of the most celebrated traffics on the Shroppie in latter years was Thomas Clayton's oil run from Stanlow on the banks of the Mersey to Langley Green, near Oldbury in the Black Country. The contract commenced in 1924 and the Clayton boats, with their characteristic decked holds, and river names, were a mainstay of trade on the canal for thirty years. Even post-war, a thousand boat-loads per annum were being despatched from Stanlow, some remaining horse-drawn until the early Fifties. But, in common with other canals, the Shropshire Union lost its final freights to the motor lorry; then, for many, with the disappearance of its working boats, something died on the Shroppie, some intangible component of canal heritage that no amount of preservation, nor hectic holiday trade, can ever quite compensate for.

On the outskirts of Nantwich the canal passes beneath the Crewe to Shrewsbury railway line. From Bridge 90 the waymarked Nantwich Riverside Loop provides an alternative means of reaching the town on foot.

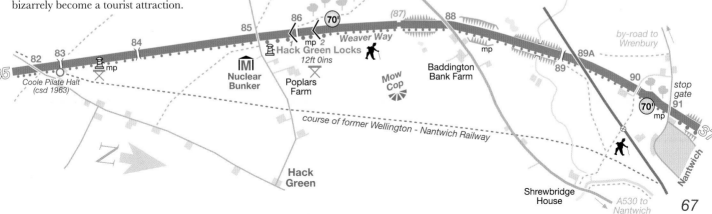

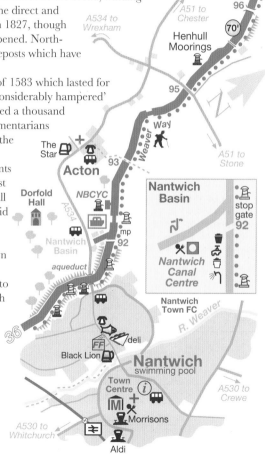

THE character of the Shropshire Union Canal changes perceptibly at Nantwich: northwards lie the broad, winding waters of its earlier constituent, the Chester Canal, opened in 1779; southwards the direct and narrow Birmingham & Liverpool Junction Canal, upon which work began here in 1827, though five years elapsed before the embankment settled sufficiently for the canal to be opened. Northbound, it's easy to feel lost without the reassuringly regular appearance of those elegant mileposts which have accompanied you from Autherley.

Long before the advent of the canals, Nantwich was reduced to ashes by the Great Fire of 1583 which lasted for almost three weeks. Four bears, thoughtfully released for their own safety, are said to have 'considerably hampered' attempts to douse the flames! Concerned for the area's salt industry, Queen Elizabeth donated a thousand pounds towards the town's rebuilding fund. Sixty years later Nantwich sided with the Parliamentarians during the Civil War, the only Cheshire town to do so. In 1644 its citizens were besieged by the Royalists for six weeks. An annual re-enactment celebrates their relief on the 25th January.

The broad embankment elevates the canal above the housing, back gardens and allotments which constitute the periphery of Nantwich. Ironically, these earthworks, together with a cast iron aqueduct over the Chester road, could have been avoided if the owners of Dorfold Hall had not objected to the passage of the canal across their land. A Sculpture Trail has been laid out beside the embankment's refurbished towpath, the main exhibit being in the form of a boat horse built out of reclaimed lock gates. Visitor moorings are provided along the length of the embankment, and they make for a pleasant overnight stay with easy access to the town centre, an enjoyable ten minutes stroll to the east.

The basin and former terminus of the Chester Canal, hints at the more expedient route to the south which Telford would have liked to have used. Nowadays it's pretty choc-a-bloc with boats, but there's a certain pleasure to be had from manoeuvring in and out of its narrow confines to get a pump-out or fill up with diesel: all a far cry from 1939 when Tom and Angela Rolt couldn't get *Cressy* into the basin because a bar of silt, built up by the passage of motor boats, prevented their entry. Adjoining the basin are the premises of the Nantwich & Border Counties Yachting Club, an organisation whose founder members were early advocates of the use of the canal system for leisure.

Between Nantwich and Hurleston Junction (Map 38) the former Chester Canal passes uneventfully through a landscape typical of the Cheshire Plain.

Nantwich Map 37

North or south, there are few English towns of this size nicer than Nantwich. The octagonal tower of St Mary's church, glimpsed across freshly-built rooftops from the high canal embankment, tempts you to moor and get to know this picturesque and historic Cheshire town. Walking in from the basin, the aqueduct forms an appropriate portcullis, and the appeal of the town increases as the centre is reached. Welsh Row is a handsome thoroughfare: keep your eyes peeled for the Tollemache Almshouses, Cheshire Constabulary police houses, Primitive Methodist chapel and Town Well House (No.52). In medieval times Nantwich was the chief salt producing town in the county.

Eating & Drinking

AUSTINS - Hospital Street. Tel: 01270 625491. Consciously old fashioned coffee house which transcends kitsch by virtue of its range of comfort food including their very own bangers and mash, cottage pie, omelettes, cakes. Open Tue, Thur, Fri & Sat 10am to 3.30pm; Wed 10am to noon. CW5 5RL
BLACK LION - Welsh Row. Tel: 01270 628711. *Good Beer Guide* recommended 17th century half-timbered pub on way into town. Weetwood ales from nearby Tarporley. CW5 5ED
CAFE DE PARIS - Hospital Street. Tel: 01270 620180. Charming oasis of an establishment run, not by a Parisian, but by a gentleman from Orleans. Coffees, soups, baguettes, French pastries and light lunches. CW5 5RP
ROMAZZINO - Love Lane (off Pillory Street). Tel: 01270 626456. Well appointed Italian restaurant open for lunch and dinner daily. CW5 5BH
If you're making the mistake of not going into town, there's a nice little cafe at Nantwich Canal Centre.

Shopping

More affluent than Market Drayton, Nantwich's antique shops and boutiques emphasise its position

at the centre of a Gucci-heeled hinterland. Keep a tight rein on your womenfolk - without firm male guidance they will run amok in Nantwich's fine clothes, shoes, and household goods outlets. But it is perhaps the food sellers that are most satisfying: butchers like Clewlows (in our top six canal-connected purveyors of pork pies), bakers like Chatwins (whose headquarters are in the town) and fishmongers like Sea Breezes all of whom have outlets in Pepper Street. Nantwich Bookshop overlooks the Town Square and is an excellent independent with

a pavement cafe and/or coffee lounge where you can dip into any newly acquired reading matter. On Hospital Street are A.T. Welch's surprisingly narrow yet deep premises housing butcher, grocer, delicatessen and coffee merchant counters which reinvent themselves, at the far end, into Austins retro coffee shop - see Eating & Drinking. The indoor market hall is open on Tuesdays, Thursdays and Saturdays, and features an eclectic range of stalls. There are Morrisons and Aldi supermarkets. Laundry facilities are available at the canal basin.

Things to Do

TOURIST INFORMATION - Civic Hall. Tel: 01270 537359. CW5 5DG
NANTWICH MUSEUM - Pillory Street. Tel: 01270 627104. Local history. Free admission. CW5 5BQ

Connections

BUSES - Arriva service 84 connects quarter-hourly Mon-Sat (hourly Sun) with Crewe (though not directly with the railway station) in one direction and half-hourly (hourly Sun) with Chester in the other with useful stops at Hurleston, Barbridge, Wardle and Calveley for towpath walkers. Tel: 0871 200 2233.
TRAINS - services to/from Crewe and Shrewsbury via Wrenbury and Whitchurch. Tel: 08457 484950.
TAXIS - Direct. Tel: 01270 585000.

Acton Map 37

A short walk across the fields from Bridge 93 leads to this village whose imposing church repays investigation, for amongst the gravestones you'll come upon that of A. N. Hornby, the English cricket captain whose one-off defeat to Australia at The Oval in 1882 brought about a spoof obituary which referred to the cremated 'remains' of the English game being sent to Australia, hence the origin of 'The Ashes'.
THE STAR - Tel: 01270 627296. 17th century half-timbered inn mentioned in *Narrow Boat*, but closed and 'For Sale' when we last passed. CW5 8LD

HURLESTON and Barbridge are the 'Clapham Junctions' of the inland waterways. Throughout the cruising season the section between them is often frenetic with boats converging and diverging to and from all points of the canal compass. Providentially the old Chester Canal was built to barge dimensions and there is usually plenty of room to manoeuvre. Bridge 98 used to carry the weight of milking herds bound for the neighbouring parlour. Now this has been converted into housing and the pastures given over to maize; a sobering reflection on the profit & loss of agriculture.

Hurleston Junction, with its quartet of locks, is the starting point of the Llangollen Canal's serene journey into Wales; a route fully covered in our *Welsh Waters Canal Companion*. It's overlooked by a high-banked reservoir which receives its water supplies from the Llangollen Canal, a factor instrumental in the survival of the waterway back in 1944 when there were proposals to close it.

Barbridge Junction marks the beginning and end of the Middlewich Branch of the Shropshire Union Canal, and it is, along with Middlewich, Great Haywood and Autherley, a pivotal point for all Four Counties Ring travellers.

On this map we include the length of canal up to Bunbury simply for the benefit of boaters journeying to or from the boatyard there. Notwithstanding the A51's thundering traffic, Barbridge is a popular overnight mooring spot, with two pubs vying for custom. And there's the interest of the junction itself, where once a transhipment shed spanned the main line. You can detect its site where the canal narrows just south of the junction. Rebuilding it would be a worthwhile heritage project.

The Texan crime writer Deborah Crombie's novel, *Water Like a Stone*, is convincingly set in and around Barbridge and Nantwich and contains a good many canal related scenes.

Summary of Facilities

Two pubs border the canal: the Olde Barbridge Inn (Tel: 01270 528327 - CW5 6AY) at Bridge 100, and the Jolly Tar (Tel: 01270 528707 - CW5 6BE), opposite the junction. There is a Countrywide store at Wardle (Tel: 01829 262677 - CW6 9GT) and the cheese merchants J. S. Bailey run a well-stocked shop and cafe at Calveley (Tel: 01829 262900 - CW6 9JW). Arriva bus service 84 runs half-hourly (hourly Sun) from stops at Hurleston, Wardle & Calveley linking Chester and Crewe via Nantwich. Tel: 0871 200 2233.

Shropshire Union Canal to Chester

Llangollen Canal to Ellesmere and Llangollen

A51

Hurleston Locks 34ft 3ins

reservoir

37

97

Hurleston Junction

99

100

Midway Boats

1

2

4 COUNTIES RING

39

Barbridge

Barbridge Inn

Jolly Tar

Barbridge Junction

101

Wardle

102

103

103A

Countrywide

104

Calveley Mill (cheese shop/cafe) coal merchant

Calveley (closed 1960)

Calveley

A51

Anglo Welsh

70'

Bunbury Staircase Locks 15ft 7ins

P

It's dispiriting to see how the towpath has been allowed to deteriorate after extensive refurbishment in the early 1990s. Why bother with improvements unless they can be maintained? Budgets slashed one imagines!

39 SUC MIDDLEWICH BRANCH Cholmondeston 4mls/2lks/2hrs

REMOTE, and seemingly always windswept, the Middlewich Branch of the Shropshire Union cuts across the grain of the landscape on a series of high embankments. It can be a busy length of canal for, as well as Four Counties Ring traffic, it funnels boats to and from the hugely popular Llangollen Canal, consequently its four deep and heavy-gated locks can become bottlenecks at the beginning and end of summer weeks.

Historically, the branch, opened in 1833, belonged to the Chester Canal Company and was engineered by Thomas Telford. Trade was heavy in cargo-carrying days, as after opening of the Birmingham & Liverpool Junction Canal this became the optimum route between the Black Country and the industrial North-west. Trade also developed between Ellesmere Port on the banks of the Mersey and The Potteries: Cornish china clay in one direction, finished crockery in the other.

In 1888 a curious experiment was undertaken, to see if it was feasible to replace horse-power by laying a narrow gauge railway along the towpath below Cholmondeston Lock, and employing a small steam locomotive called 'Dickie' to haul strings of narrowboats. The concept didn't develop here, laying track was considered cost-prohibitive and there were problems in steering the boats, though it did catch on abroad, especially on the French waterways. Cholmondeston still retains a railway presence, however, in the shape of the Crewe to Chester line, part of the historic route of the Irish Mails to Holyhead.

A high wooded embankment carries the canal across the River Weaver. Four Counties Ring travellers meet the river again near Audlem. It rises on the south-facing slopes of the Peckforton Hills and passes beneath the Llangollen Canal at Wrenbury prior to becoming navigable at Winsford, less than five miles downstream of the Weaver Aqueduct. There is nothing spectacular about the canal's crossing of the river, but it takes place in the most agreeable of locations. And, as you pass on your elevated way, it's hard to escape a fleeting sense of regret that the riverbank, being on private land, cannot so easily be explored.

Summary of Facilities

Two marinas - one long established, the other brand new - provide the only facilities available on the Middlewich Branch. They are, respectively: VENETIAN MARINA (Tel: 01270 - 528538 CW5 6DD) and AQUEDUCT MARINA (Tel: 01270 525041 CW5 6DX). The latter features The Galley cafe/restaurant open daily from 9.30am and offering evening meals on Fridays and Saturdays. Tel: 01270 525043.

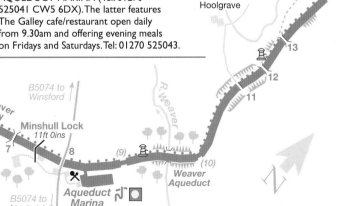

TO subconsciously relegate the Middlewich Branch to the back of your mind as an unspectacular, but necessary link in the waterways of the North-West would be unjust, for this is a rumbustious canal, extrovertly ushering you loftily above the snaking valley of the Weaver, presenting you with expansive views towards a horizon bounded by Delamere Forest and the Peckforton Hills. Church Minshull - all russet coloured brick and black & white half timbering - looks, from the canal's elevated position, like a toy village embracing the river's luxuriant banks. Tom and Angela Rolt enjoyed an extended stay here in the fateful Autumn of 1939 while Tom worked for Rolls Royce at Crewe. It was tedious work he didn't enjoy, but the couple revelled in the close-knit community which flourished at Minshull: the blacksmith who shod the local cart horses; and the miller whose water wheels supplied the village with its electricity, continuing to do so right up until 1960.

Several sizeable farms border the canal, their fields filled with dairy herds or cut red by the plough in a ruddy shade of corduroy. The cattle appear not averse to drinking canal water. In a belated attempt to derive much needed extra income, British Waterways experimented with fitting individual monitoring devices to cows known by the acronym BUMS, short for bovine utilisation monitoring systems. Near Bridge 22, woods partially obscure the Top Flash, a subsidence induced lake beside the Weaver. The main London-Glasgow railway crosses the canal, its sleek electric trains swishing by at forty times the speed of your boat. To the south-east lies a forgotten, older transport route, a Roman road which linked the early salt mines at Nantwich and Middlewich. Some interesting old canal horse stables have been converted into living quarters by Bridge 18.

The Middlewich Branch's towpath is largely grassy: fine for well-shod walkers but horribly bumpy and uncomfortable for cycling until it reaches Clive Green, east of which it has been upgraded as part of National Cycleway No.5.

Summary of Facilities

The Badger Inn at Church Minshull (Tel: 01270 522348 - CW5 6DY) is a smartly refurbished country inn (easily reached from Bridge 14) offering food and accommodation and open from 11.30am daily (noon Sun). Arriva bus service 31A operates hourly Mon-Sat from Church Minshull to Crewe. Tel: 0871 200 2233.

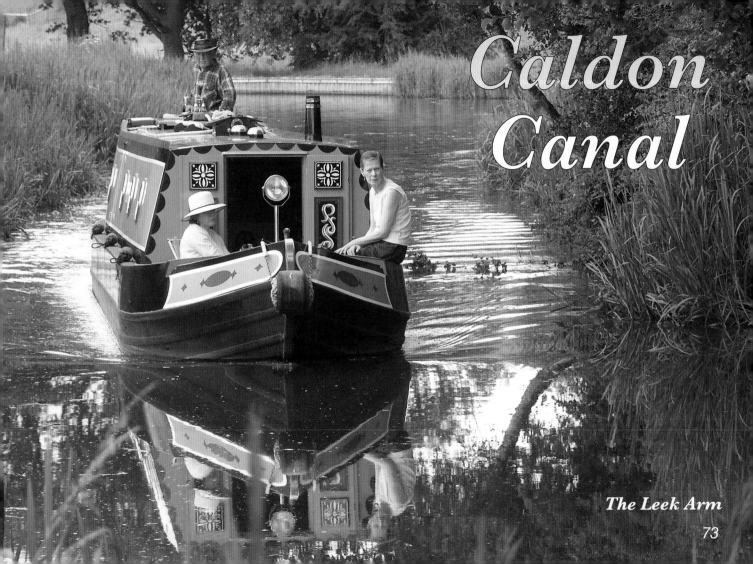

Caldon
Canal

The Leek Arm

41 CALDON CANAL Stockton Brook 5mls/6lks/3hrs

RUNNING south to north through the upper valley of the Trent - a narrow, lacklustre stream difficult to equate with the river that this guide encounters at Derwent Mouth - the Caldon Canal struggles to extricate itself from the urbanisation of The Potteries. When fields do finally appear they seem shaggy and unkempt, as though this were a war-torn no-man's land between true countryside and town. Just before Milton a short arm once led to Ford Green ironworks and Smallthorne Colliery, both long vanished. Milton is a popular overnight mooring point, with useful shopping and eating & drinking opportunities easily accessed. Whilst here you may care to enrol at the canalside Hardman Football Development Centre, an organisation obviously determined to correct what they see as a worrying trend towards the softening up of what was once regarded as a contact sport.

Engine Lock recalls the existence of a pumping engine in the vicinity of Cockshead Colliery. The chamber is one of the deepest on the system. There was once a busy boatbuilding yard here. At Norton Green the Knypersley Feeder (at one time navigable, if you can credit it, to basins serving Cockshead Colliery and Cope's Iron Foundry) joins the canal. Knypersley is one of three reservoirs, along with Stanley and Rudyard, which feed into the Caldon, and thence the Trent & Mersey. The fledgling Trent, a hundred and seventy miles upstream of its union with the Humber, is piped beneath the canal by Bridge 22.

The Stockton Brook flight carries the canal forty feet up to its summit level of 486ft. The waterworks at the foot of the flight was built by the Staffordshire Potteries Water Co. in 1884 and once contained a pair of horizontal compound tandem 'Davey' differential steam engines. Decommissioned some time ago, the works awaits a new use to be found for it. Attractive ceramic sculptures adorn locks 6 and 7. They are the work of Anthony Lysycia who has also provided canalside artworks at Hatton, Trevor and Llanymynech. 'The Knotty's' Stoke to Leek line crosses the canal between the second and third lock. Disused since the 1990s, a business known as Moorland & City Railways has aspirations of restoring the line so the quarries at Cauldon Lowe and the theme park at Alton Towers can be linked to the rest of the railway network at Stoke. In another initiative, Staffordshire County Council have invested £2.5m in upgrading the towpath between Stockton Brook and Leek and Cheddleton. It's part of the Pedal Peak cycle route, and a very good job they've made of it too, with a firm all weather, but not overly 'municipal', surface of compacted stone.

⚠ Beware low headroom at Bridge 18
Lift-bridges 21 and 23 require the use of a windlass

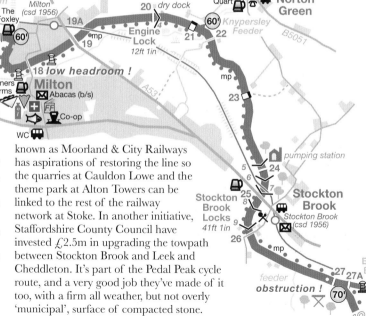

74

Stone walls and small holdings begin to create a Pennine sense of obduracy. When we first knew this stretch of canal back in the late 1970s, you could count on seeing a water vole paddling across from one bank to another. Now you are more likely to see mink. Before Bridge 27 an unusual circular metal platform obstructs the centre of the channel, marking the site of a light-railway swing-bridge. Endon Basin, once used as a transhipment point from rail to canal for Cauldon Lowe limestone, is now occupied by Stoke-on-Trent Boat Club whose members were strong advocates for the retention of the Caldon Canal when it was threatened with abandonment in the 1960s. From Bridge 27 a footpath can be followed to Stanley Pool. Mileposts along the A53 bear more than a passing resemblance to those on the canal.

Milton   Map 41

Milton is a lively little frontier post, a last chance for human contact and meaningful shopping until you reach Leek - always assuming you're going that way - and its facilities become even more significant if you're heading off into the sequestered folds of the Churnet Valley. Just west of Bridge 18 an interpretive board celebrates the pottery designer Susie Cooper (1902-1995).

Eating & Drinking

THE FOXLEY - Foxley Lane. Tel: 01782 536641. Much improved canalside pub with offside moorings but no direct access from the towpath. ST2 7EH

MINERS ARMS - Millrise Road (east of Bridge 18 on way into village centre). Tel: 01782 545510. ST2 7DW

MILTON FRYER - Leek Road. Tel: 01782 214897. Friendly chippy which has been 'frying' since 1947. ST1 6HD

Shopping

There are two butchers (that nearer the canal also being a bakery) a pharmacy, off-licence, greengrocer/farmshop (Tel: 01782 570330), Nisa and Co-op with a cash machine. Abacas (Tel: 01782 543005) is a splendid secondhand bookshop with a wide-ranging stock and a nice line in new North Staffordshire publications and greetings cards.

Connections

BUSES - First Potteries service 43 runs at 20 minute intervals (hourly Sun) to/from Hanley. Tel: 0871 200 2233

Norton Green   Map 41

Self-styled (with justification) as 'the first village on the River Trent'. Hugh Bourne (1772-1852), co-founder of the Primitive Methodists, lived at nearby Bemersley Green.

Eating & Drinking

THE FOAMING QUART - Tel: 01782 911171. Quaint Marston's pub (8 mins walk from Br. 21) which Eric Bristow represented when winning the World Darts Championship in 1983. Open from noon. ST6 8PD

Connections

BUSES - variants of the number 8 run at frequent intervals to/from Hanley. Tel: 0871 200 2233.

Endon Meadowsweet

Stockton Brook   Map 41

Wayside community on the main road between Hanley and Leek. The former timber-built station building houses a firm specialising in fitted kitchens and bathrooms.

Eating & Drinking

THE SPORTSMAN - Tel: 01782 505307. Stone-built Marston's local adjoining Bridge 25. ST9 9NT

THE HOLLYBUSH - Tel: 01782 502116. Ego Mediterranean restaurant & bar. ST9 9NL

Shopping

Post office: also sells bread, milk and newspapers etc.

Connections

BUSES - First service 18 runs every 20 minutes (hourly Sun) to/from Hanley and Leek. Tel: 0871 200 2233.

Endon   Map 42

Endon - known for its Whitsun 'well dressing' - boasts a pharmacy and convenience store (from which swipe cards for the facilities at Park Lane Wharf are obtainable) handy for the visitor moorings by Bridge 28. On the A53 there's a Toby Carvery and a pub.

Denford   Map 42

THE HOLLY BUSH - canalside Bridge 38. Tel: 01538 371819. Something of an institution with locals, boaters and walkers alike, this comfortable and beautifully situated canalside pub is now owned by Thwaites of Lancaster and food is served from noon daily. ST13 7JT

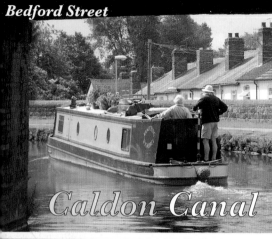

Bedford Street

Caldon Canal

James Brindley

Hanley Bottle Kilns

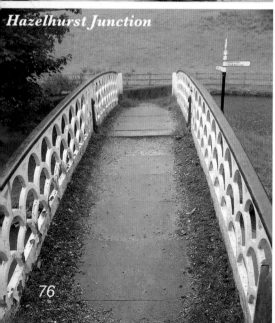

Hazelhurst Junction

Hazelhurst Aqueduct

Turnover Bridge 52

Black Lion

Consall Forge Canoes

Tunnel Pool

ARCING around Endon, the Caldon Canal heads for Hazelhurst Junction. There is no more sublime a meeting or parting of waterways on the whole canal system. If, on arrival, you experience a sense of deja vu, then cast your mind back to Hardings Wood where the Macclesfield performs an equally acrobatic manoeuvre in departing the Trent & Mersey as the short Leek Branch does here. It wasn't always so. Originally the Caldon descended to the valley floor from Endon. Then, with construction of the Leek Branch, the new line we use today was built, with a staircase lock forming an abrupt descent adjacent to Bridge 3 at Denford. But the staircase was a bottleneck for the heavy traffic of limestone boats from

see enlargement page 80

unnavigable feeder from Rudyard

Country Park

aqueduct

The Roaches

Longsdon

Wall Grange Farm

Leek Tunnel
130 yards

Leekbrook Junction

Staffs Way

Leek Branch

Cheddleton Heath

Endon

Toby Carvery

Park Lane Wharf

original course of Caldon Canal

Hazelhurst Locks 10-12
25ft 10ins

Denford
aqueducts

former asylum

R. Churnet

Endon (csd 1956)

Hazelhurst Junction

site of staircase locks

Country Park

Wall Grange (csd 1956)

for details of facilities at Endon and Denford turn back to page 75

cricket ground

Froghall, and so in 1841 the present layout was arrived at, with three single chambers taking the main line down under a new aqueduct, which carried the Leek branch and Rudyard feeder; ensuring that the latter joined the main canal, of necessity, at its summit level. History apart, the whole canal configuration is thoroughly exciting, and makes for a hugely enjoyable 'figure of eight' towpath stroll centred on the "Hollybush Inn" at Denford.

Beyond Denford the Caldon's Main Line passes through the glorious environment of Deep Hayes Country Park where there are offside moorings for visiting boaters. Turning south-eastwards, the canal enters the Churnet Valley. Enclosed by high ridges, it reaches Cheddleton where a delightful flint mill, powered by twin waterwheels, graces the scene. In the past there were also limekilns, silk and paper mills and a brewery here. Again the canalscape is full of appeal. A plaque by Cheddleton top lock marks the re-opening of the Caldon Canal in 1974 after it had fallen into dereliction in the early 1960s. No one should pass this point without mouthing a silent 'thank you' to the waterway enthusiasts and local authorities who 'engineered' this magical canal's restoration.

Staffs Way

Flint Mill

industrial units

Cheddleton Locks
16ft 2ins

Churnet Valley Railway

Cheddleton

The Boat

Wood's Lock
5ft 3ins
sewage works

figures refer to main line, allow 1 hour to cruise Leek Branch (one way).

for details of facilities at Leek and Cheddleton turn to page 80

*Taking the Leek Branch
at Hazelhurst Junction*

The Leek Arm

From Hazelhurst, the branch to Leek curves away from the main line which locks attractively down to pass beneath it. Two overbridges precede a sharp turn at the site of the old staircase locks before the branch then crosses the main line on an imposing brick aqueduct dated 1841. A lesser aqueduct over the railway follows before the branch settles down on the opposite hillside for the delightful journey to Leek. Winding, dipping in and out of overbridges, and passing some envy-provoking waterside properties, the canal traverses a gorgeous belt of woodland, full of bluebells in spring, where jays screech jocularly amongst the tree tops and brackeny banks spill down into the valley of the River Churnet. Presently the view ahead opens out towards the high flanks of The Morridge rising to 1,300ft in the east, whilst glowering over your right-hand shoulder stands the spooky tower of St Edward's, the former county mental asylum. If the inmates weren't deranged before they were incarcerated here, they would probably be sent mad by the sheer despondency of the hospital's grim institutional architecture, ironically now transformed into exclusive housing.

All of a sudden the canal encounters a remote pool enclosed by low hills - one of the most idyllic mooring spots on the whole system. The canal builders had no alternative but to dig a tunnel in order to reach Leek. The confined 130 yard bore is fronted by an ornate portal of red sandstone. Walkers take the horsepath across the top and are rewarded by stunning views over the town to The Roaches beyond.

Less than a mile of canal remains in water. The final full size winding hole is just beyond Bridge 9. We just managed to navigate a 45ft boat to the shallow end of the canal and turned it with some difficulty, but essentially, the canal peters out as its feeder comes in from Rudyard, three miles to the north. A public footpath (part of the Staffordshire Way) follows the feeder to the reservoir which gave us Kipling's Christian name. An aqueduct, dated 1801, once carried the canal across the Churnet to reach a terminal wharf nearer the town centre. The aqueduct remains but is bereft of water, whilst the bed of the canal lies beneath an industrial estate. An irreversible loss to this now tourist-conscious town.

Leek

Map 42

Full of sudden architectural treats, Leek is tucked away from the outside world in deep folds of the Staffordshire Moorlands and is an entertaining and evocative place to explore. Canal travellers are thus entitled to mourn the disappearance of the old terminal arm and the resultant bleak trudge through an industrial estate to reach the town centre. Perseverance brings its rewards, however, and you'll soon find yourself warming to Leek, much as William Morris did on his frequent visits to Wardle's dyeworks. The Nicholson War Memorial is of poignant significance, a grieving father's tribute to a son lost in the First World War.

Eating & Drinking

ABDUL SPICE RESTAURANT - Stockwell Street. Tel: 01538 373734. Indian/Bangladeshi. ST13 6DH
DEN ENGEL - Stanley Street. Tel: 01538 373751. Belgium comes to north Staffs. Leffe on tap. ST13 5DR
FOXLOWE - Market Place. Tel: 01538 386112. Comfortable art centre cafe 10-4pm daily. ST13 6AD
GETLIFFE'S - Getliffe Yard (off Derby Street). Tel: 01538 382812. Stylish restaurant/cafe/wine bar with alfresco eating opportunities on cobbled courtyard. Open Mon-Wed 10am-4pm, Thur-Sat 9.30am-11pm. ST13 6HU
LEEK OATCAKE SHOP - Haywood Street. Tel: 01538 387556. A mandatory pilgrimage for filled oatcakes. Open from the crack of dawn daily ex Mon. ST13 5JX
PRIMA PIANO - Sheep Street. Tel: 01538 398289. Italian restaurant. ST13 5HW.
WHITE HART - Stockwell Street. Tel: 01538 372122. Tea room with sun-kissed courtyard. ST13 6DH

Shopping

All facilities can be found in the town centre a mile north-east of the canal, though there is a large Morrisons supermarket nearer at hand. The outdoor retail market is held on Wednesdays (flea market Sats) but the charming little indoor Butter Market additionally functions on Fridays and Saturdays. The delight of shopping in Leek lies in the proliferation of

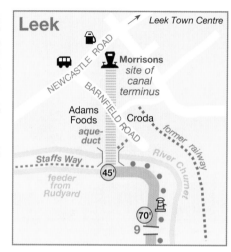

small shops offering individuality and personal service such as Pronto in Sheepmarket Street, a lively delicatessen and eatery. There is a Fine Food Market on the third Saturday in the month, and a good new/secondhand bookshop (closed Mon) on Stanley Street. Leek is also enjoying a burgeoning reputation as a centre for the antiques trade.

Things to Do

TOURIST INFORMATION/NICHOLSON MUSEUM & ART GALLERY - Stockwell Street. Tel: 01538 483741. Open Mon-Sat 10am-4pm, admission free. Local history and travelling exhibitions housed in building designed by the local Sugden architectural practice. Emphasis given to the Leek Embroidery School. ST13 6DW
BRINDLEY MILL/MUSEUM - Mill Street. Small admission charge. Open Easter- September Sat, Sun & BH Mons 2-5pm. Open same hours Mons, Tues & Weds in late July/August. Restored water powered corn mill built by James Brindley in 1752. ST13 8AF

Connections

BUSES - rather sadly, the erstwhile independents Procters and Clowes have pulled out of stage buses, leaving the field to First supported by Wardle. First Potteries service 18 operates every 20 minutes Mon-Sat to/from Hanley via Endon (hourly Sun) and will whisk you up the hill to the town centre if you're not minded to walk. Wardle's service 16 provides a link with Cheddleton whilst their 234/5/6 runs to/from Cheadle via Froghall. Service 423/4 provides a limited link (Mon-Fri) with Rudyard offering the opportunity for a one-way walk along the feeder. Tel: 0871 200 2233.
TAXIS - Malkins. Tel: 01538 386797.

Cheddleton

Map 42

Interesting village (St Edward's church has some fine Pre-Raphaelite glass) offering shopping and refreshment opportunities before you head into the interior.

Eating & Drinking

BOAT INN - Basford Bridge Lane (Bridge 44). Tel: 01538 360683. Canalside Marston's pub. ST13 7EQ
CASTROS - Cheadle Road (Bridge 42). Tel: 01538 361500. Mexican restaurant open from 6pm Tue-Sat. ST13 7HN
OLD SCHOOL TEA ROOM - Hollow Lane. Tel: 01538 360340. Splendid tea room and gift shop (Wed-Sun, 10am-4pm) about quarter of an hour's walk up past the church.

Shopping

Off licence, convenience store and pharmacy half a mile up the hill from the canal, and a post office by Bridge 42.

Things to Do

CHEDDLETON FLINT MILL - one of the great little museums of England. Tel: 0161 408 5083. ST13 7HL
CHURNET VALLEY RAILWAY - operates Sats, Suns, Bank Hol Mons, and Weds in Jul & Aug. Tel: 01538 750755. Preserved railway evoking much nostalgia plus an excellent way to facilitate a one-way towpath walk. Excursions on selected dates to Cauldon Lowe. ST13 7EE

Connections

BUSES - service 16 operates hourly Mon-Fri and bi-hourly Sat & Sun to/from Leek and Hanley. Tel: 0871 200 2233.

43 CALDON CANAL Consall Forge & Froghall 4mls/2lks/2hrs

BEYOND Cheddleton the enchantment deepens as the Caldon engenders an almost Amazonian sense of solitude: a blur of butterbur and balsam; meadowsweet and willowherb. Briefly, in a distant echo of the arrangement at Alrewas (Map 16) the canal merges with the River Churnet at Oakmeadow Ford Lock, though there is little change of character, other than when heavy rainfall causes the river current to increase its normally sluggish pace - check the gauge at Bridge 48 to ensure that it is sensible to proceed.

You begin to wonder why on earth they ever bothered to build a canal in such an extraordinarily remote outpost of Staffordshire. But this is a countryside with plenty of skeletons in its closet. Haematite iron ore and limestone were extensively mined in the area, and there were also several coal shafts and flint-grinding mills. At its zenith in the 1860s, an average of thirty boats a day were carrying ore out of the Churnet Valley.

The Caldon Canal was promoted for two main reasons: for the export of limestone from Cauldon (sic) Lowe; and to provide the summit of the Trent & Mersey with extra water. It opened in 1779, but was literally the death of James Brindley, who caught pneumonia on a surveying trip with fatal consequences for that genius of the early canal era.

Reaching Consall Forge, the river disengages itself from the canal, disappearing over a weir to race ahead down the valley. The canal, however, makes light of this snub, passing under the railway, once a picturesque byway of the North Staffordshire Railway, now a preserved line of considerable charm.

The channel grows noticeably more slender, so that the passing of oncoming boats becomes a matter of discretion and a little 'give and take'. Squeezing past the cantilevered waiting room of Consall's beautifully restored station, the canal runs parallel to the railway, encountering a row of redbrick railway workers houses looking incongruously suburban in so bucolic a setting. Milepost 15 appears to be on the wrong side of the canal, but apparently the towpath ran along the opposite bank before the railway came along. A lofty conifer stands guard over Flint Mill Lock, at which point the captains of craft over 65ft have to consider whether they are likely to be able to squeeze through Froghall Tunnel or not. The biblical metaphor concerning camels and eyes of needles springs to mind. Consall Mills, long retired from manual labour, are another reminder of the valley's past industry.

A little curiosity catches the eye on the towpath side between the tail of Flint Mill Lock and turnover Bridge 52. 'Tickle Ridge' is a layer of limestone created by liquid lime deposits running down the hillside over the centuries, the Churnet Valley's equivalent, perhaps, of Mother Shipton's Well at Knaresborough.

Cherry Eye Bridge recalls, it is said,

continued overleaf:

81

continued from page 81:

the inflamed, bloodshot eyes of the neighbourhood's ironstone workers. Its Gothic pointed arch would not look out of place in the nave of a parish church. The Staffordshire Way leaves the canal in the vicinity of milepost 16, duplicated by one of the original stone mileposts.

A concreted section of canal follows as an embanked length prone to breaching is negotiated. Woodland tumbles down to the water's edge on one side, whilst on the other, an equally steep descent leads to the Churnet. Suddenly a factory wall looms out of the trees, heralding the formerly vast copper wire works of Thomas Bolton & Sons. The factory dates from 1890 and once operated a small fleet of narrowboats, though most of its transport needs were supplied by the railway. It was turned over to munitions during the war and apparently the Luftwaffe tried to bomb it but couldn't find it; which is not surprising when you take into account its position in this amphitheatre of heavily wooded hills. Much of the site has been demolished and nothing done to fill the void.

Many boats won't fit into Froghall Tunnel ... but then again, given Britain's record levels of obesity, neither, perhaps, will many boaters. A 65ft winding hole is provided for boats unable to negotiate the tunnel, but if your boat conformed to the loading gauge (roughly five feet square above the water line) at Flint Mill Lock, you can proceed to the picturesque terminus which lies beyond. The rest of us (whatever our girth) must plod along the path around the side; though, enviously, we watched three mallard ducks glide insouciantly through.

The peace and quiet of Froghall Basin today is hard to reconcile with the busy site where limestone, brought down by plate tramway from the quarries, was cut to size and loaded on to narrowboats. Here were sidings, great banks of limestone, smoking kilns, and, significantly, the top lock of the Uttoxeter extension, opened in 1811. It proved financially unviable and when the North Staffordshire Railway acquired the Trent & Mersey system they quickly closed it down and built a railway over much of its thirteen mile course. Now, of course, the railway has gone the way of the canal, though it has been converted into a delightful bridleway between Oakamoor and Denstone. A feasibility study has been published with a long term view to re-opening the Uttoxeter Canal, but in some respects it would be a shame to disturb this secret valley all over again.

At Froghall, the top lock has been refurbished to provide access to a mooring basin, though little use appears to be made of this. Over seventy-five years have passed since the wharf was abandoned commercially, and in the intervening period nature has reclaimed what she obviously regards as rightfully her own.

Consall Forge   Map 43

Peace and tranquillity characterise Consall to such an extent now that it is hard to visualise the activity of the forges, furnaces and slitting mills which clustered here in the seventeenth and eighteenth centuries. Consall Forge Pottery (between bridges 50b and 51 - Tel: 01538 266625) produces hand-thrown domestic stoneware.

Eating & Drinking
BLACK LION - Consall Forge. Tel: 01782 550294. One of the most delightfully located pubs on the inland waterway system. Pub grub and real ales. ST9 0AJ
Things to Do
CONSALL HALL GARDENS - Consall. Tel: 01782 749994. Seventy acres of landscaped gardens, lakes and follies. Open Weds, Suns and BHs, 10am to 5pm, Easter to October. Gift shop and tearoom. Access from the canal at Consall forge, approx 1 mile. ST9 0AG

Froghall   Map 43

The copper wire works continues to shrink and, as yet, the wastelands which have taken its place have not been redeveloped; *thankfully* one might suggest. The 328ft high chimney, threatened with demolition, has been saved as a landmark, for the time being at least. Incidentally, copper cable from Bolton's sister factory at nearby Oakamoor was laid across the ocean bed to form the first Transatlantic telegraph in 1866. Sadly the trip boat *Birdswood* has ceased operating and refreshments are no longer obtainable from the wharf house. The Country Rangers information office is open, however, at weekends.

Eating & Drinking
RAILWAY INN - Tel: 01538 752863. Food and bed & breakfast beside the railway station. ST10 2HA
Things to Do
CHURNET VALLEY RAILWAY - as Cheddleton. Tea room and souvenir shop on Froghall station open on operating days. ST10 2HA
KINGSLEY BIRD & FALCONRY CENTRE - Sprinks Lane, Kingsley (access via Staffordshire Way from Cherry Eye Bridge. Tel: 01538 754784. Tea room. ST10 2BX
Connections
BUSES - Wardle's 234/5/6 offers a Monday to Saturday service linking Froghall (stop by railway bridge) with Cheadle (a nice little town dominated by Pugin's fabulously ornate Catholic church) in one direction and Leek in the other. Tel: 0871 200 2233.

Weaver Navigation

Vale Royal Lock

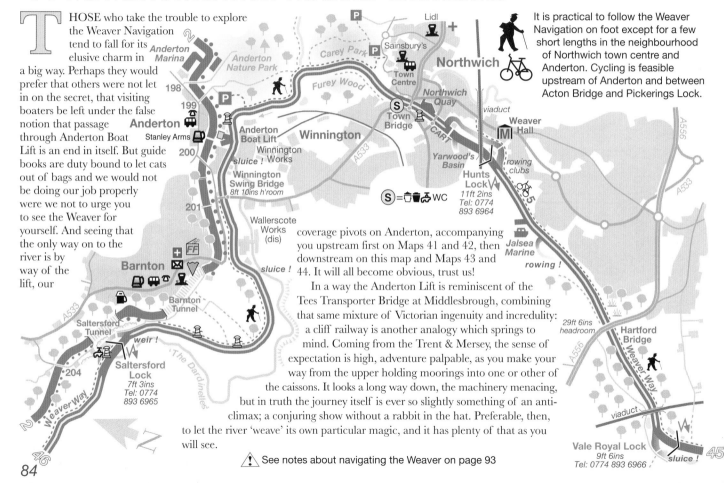

THOSE who take the trouble to explore the Weaver Navigation tend to fall for its elusive charm in a big way. Perhaps they would prefer that others were not let in on the secret, that visiting boaters be left under the false notion that passage through Anderton Boat Lift is an end in itself. But guide books are duty bound to let cats out of bags and we would not be doing our job properly were we not to urge you to see the Weaver for yourself. And seeing that the only way on to the river is by way of the lift, our

It is practical to follow the Weaver Navigation on foot except for a few short lengths in the neighbourhood of Northwich town centre and Anderton. Cycling is feasible upstream of Anderton and between Acton Bridge and Pickerings Lock.

coverage pivots on Anderton, accompanying you upstream first on Maps 41 and 42, then downstream on this map and Maps 43 and 44. It will all become obvious, trust us!

In a way the Anderton Lift is reminiscent of the Tees Transporter Bridge at Middlesbrough, combining that same mixture of Victorian ingenuity and incredulity: a cliff railway is another analogy which springs to mind. Coming from the Trent & Mersey, the sense of expectation is high, adventure palpable, as you make your way from the upper holding moorings into one or other of the caissons. It looks a long way down, the machinery menacing, but in truth the journey itself is ever so slightly something of an anti-climax; a conjuring show without a rabbit in the hat. Preferable, then, to let the river 'weave' its own particular magic, and it has plenty of that as you will see.

⚠ See notes about navigating the Weaver on page 93

Map labels:

Anderton Marina
Anderton Nature Park
Carey Park
Lidl
Sainsbury's
Northwich
Town Centre
Furey Wood
198
199
P
Anderton
Stanley Arms
Anderton Boat Lift
Winnington
Winnington Works
200
sluice !
Winnington Swing Bridge
8ft 10ins h'room
201
Wallerscote Works (dis)
Northwich Quay
Town Bridge
viaduct
Weaver Hall
Yarwood's Basin
Hunts Lock
11ft 2ins
Tel: 0774 893 6964
rowing clubs
(S)=WC
Jalsea Marine
rowing !
Barnton
FF
Barnton Tunnel
sluice !
Saltersford Tunnel
204
weir !
The Dardinelles
Saltersford Lock
7ft 3ins
Tel: 0774 893 6965
Weaver Way
29ft 6ins headroom
Hartford Bridge
Weaver Way
viaduct
Vale Royal Lock
9ft 6ins
Tel: 0774 893 6966
sluice !
A556
A533
A5
2
46
45

Upstream

Turning upstream, the navigation seems enormously wide by Trent & Mersey standards. Immediately the Weaver's characteristically self-effacing style manifests itself, high banks emphasising the river's solitary disposition. Presently, Northwich town centre appears on the port side. £80m is being invested in the Baron's Quay development and the Town Council are keen to further enhance the river corridor, recognizing that, in this post-industrial era, they have a prize asset on their doorstep. To starboard is a Canal & River Trust services block providing water, toilets, rubbish and Elsan disposal facilities, though no longer self-pump-out.

Town is one of two hefty swing-bridges spanning the Weaver at Northwich (built, incidentally, by the Handyside Company of Derby) but both have sufficient headroom to allow most inland waterway craft to pass beneath without requiring them to be swung, though it may be a different matter for the high-masted yachts which migrate upriver for the winter. Between the swing-bridges the navigation widens into a sizeable pool: egress point of the unnavigable Dane. Here, most welcome boating facilities are provided at Northwich Quay, a secure mooring point offering both permanent and visiting boaters showers, laundry, pump-out, whilst a Waitrose supermarket stands handily alongside.

Northwich used to make a living not only from salt and chemicals, but from shipbuilding too. Several busy yards were based here turning out narrowboats, wide beam barges, tugs, coasters, river steamers and ferries. Some of the 'Brunners' were built by Yarwoods. Yarwoods also built a good many narrowboats for the Grand Union Canal Carrying Company's fleet. But perhaps one of their most curious commissions was the RAF's auxilary vessel *Aquarius* launched in 1934, a 'spy ship' whose construction was overseen by 'Lawrence of Arabia' shortly before his fatal motorcycle accident. Lamentably little remains of the half a dozen or so boat building yards which existed here in the industry's heyday.

Hunts Lock, the first of two upstream of Anderton, is framed by a

continued overleaf:

Winnington Teasels

85

continued from page 85:

high railway viaduct carrying the old Cheshire Lines Committee's route from Manchester to Chester. Archive photographs depict Hunts Lock filled with a multiplicity of craft: steam packets, Weaver flats, tugs and launches. In common with all Weaver locks there are two chambers at Hunts, the smaller being the one now regularly used. Also in evidence are the railway type signals once used to indicate the state of readiness of the locks to approaching shipping. The lock is operated by its keeper. Travelling upstream he'll probably drop you a line in the sense that he'll lower a rope for you to attach your ropes to so as to secure your boat against turbulence as the lock fills. Upstream of Hunts, the channel, by-passing old meanders, is long and relatively straight as far as the Vale Royal railway bridge. This reach is used for rowing and, with footpaths on either bank, is also popular with pedestrians. Fishermen favour this length too, finding it well stocked with good-sized roach, perch, pike, tench and bream. Jalsea Marine's yard invariably contains an interesting assortment of craft in various states of undress. The yard used to belong to Pimblotts who built 'Brunners', wide boats for the Leeds & Liverpool Canal, barges for the Bridgewater Department of the MSC, and some of the distinctive steel hulled 'Admiral' class narrowboats.

Hartford (or 'Blue') Bridge carries the frenetically busy dual-carriageway Northwich by-pass across the navigation. It is built, uninspiringly but practically, of concrete piers with a steel span. Beyond it the Weaver finally begins to justify its reputation for beauty. Trees spill down to the water's edge, their higher branches framing a lofty sand-stone viaduct built by the Grand Junction Railway in 1837 and now carrying the electrified West Coast Main Line across the Weaver Navigation. From these hurrying trains you catch tantalising glimpses of

Winsford

the Weaver luxuriating in its wooded cutting, but by water the journey is so much slower and the sense of intimacy correspondingly deeper. Set on a bend - so that, whichever way you are travelling, it remains out of sight until the last moment - Vale Royal Lock is amongst the loveliest on the inland waterways. The lock-keeper has one of those jobs you would gleefully consider murdering for. An affable cove, he is something of a bird-watcher, and lists of recent sightings adorn the window of his lockside office. If he's not too busy, ask if you can see the turbine machinery which powers the lock.

Downstream

Turn to starboard out of the Anderton Lift, and you'll find yourself heading downstream through the river's most industrial zone. Not that it can hold a candle to its commercial heyday. Forty years ago British Waterways were energetically promoting Anderton as an inland port, and not without effect, three or four ships a week coming up the Weaver with general cargoes for warehousing here. None of that remains now, and an air of sadness hangs over the deserted soda ash quays at Wallerscote, graffitied with the names of ships that have docked here in the busier past. Saltersford Lock lies within spitting distance of the Trent & Mersey Canal. Ironic, isn't it, that the Weaver, progressively invested in and modernised, should be so quiet, whereas the old canal up on the hillside, virtually unchanged since its construction in the 18th century, is hugely busy with boats. It's the automated, large chamber which boaters use at Saltersford now. The lock-keeper operates the lock for you, though he has other duties too, being called away on occasion to swing the navigation's big bridges when high-masted vessels are in the offing. There are excellent visitor moorings downstream of the lock.

45 WEAVER NAVIGATION Winsford 4mls/0lks/1.5hrs

CONNOISSEURS regard the Vale Royal Cut as the prettiest stretch of the Weaver, and their opinion is difficult to refute. The visitor moorings upstream of Vale Royal Locks must qualify as one of the most idyllic on the inland waterways network. In medieval times there was a huge Cistercian abbey hereabouts. It had been founded by King Edward I in 1277 in his gratitude for being spared on a perilous voyage back from the Holy Land. In subsidence induced flashes grebes and coots nest on floating lily pads and yellow iris are abundant. Cut your engine if you're boating, and just listen to the birdsong.

New Bridge was the scene in 1892 of riots during a prolonged waterman's strike. In the end order was restored when a crack regiment of Hussars was brought in by train from Manchester. The picnic site which exists today seems dull by comparison. Beware the swing-bridge's low headroom, it may have to be swung even for some narrow boats. The bosky charm of Vale Royal gives way to Little Siberia as the Weaver negotiates a reach overlooked by a massive rock salt mine. Five hundred feet down, its galleries extend for well over a hundred miles. The bulk of the mine's production is used for road de-icing, but its worked out seams now provide useful storage space for all manner of data, records and valuable artefacts.

Crumbling timber quays recall the Weaver's part in the transportation of mid Cheshire salt products. Two railway companies vied for this business too. The Cheshire Lines Committee called their station Winsford & Over, the London & North Western named theirs Over & Wharton. The route of the former has been converted into the Whitegate Way, a six mile long public bridleway and wildlife haven. The future will apparently be greener still, as various land reclamation projects bear fruit. Personally, though, we'd swap them all for a chance encounter with a passing coaster, like all navigations which have lost their trade it is difficult to escape an empty sense of melancholy and lack of purpose.

The town of Winsford gloomily straddles both banks of the Weaver; an industrial abyss dropped in the midst of Cheshire pastures. Colonised by post war overspill schemes, its economy now seems in the lap of baleful business parks. Winsford Bridges mark the end of the Canal & River Trust's jurisdiction of the river, but the local authority indulgently permit gratis exploration of Winsford Bottom Flash, a lake-like expanse of water brought about by subsidence resulting from salt mining. Leaving the river's confines and heading out into the flash is like going out to sea. Gulls enhance this illusion, as do the sailing dinghies. Red buoys mark the shallows, yellow buoys mark the racing zone. Local boaters will tell you that it is possible to drop your anchor and moor midstream, though you may prefer to return to the more orthodox confines of the river. At least you can secretly congratulate yourself you came and saw and conquered.

Dutton Viaduct

Frodsham Quay

Anderton Lift

Dutton Horse Bridge

88

Northwich

Surprisingly large, and unexpectedly likeable, you can tell that Northwich is off the beaten track because it still retains a good number of five figure telephone numbers. Handy moorings offer instant access to the town's pedestrianised shopping streets characterized by handsome but ersatz half-timber buildings erected to compensate for salt-mining wrought subsidence. Raise your eyes above their customary horizontality to admire the fascinating figurines which adorn the upper frontages of many black & white buildings.

Eating & Drinking
THE PENNY BLACK - Witton Street. Tel: 01606 42029. Wetherspoons housed in former post office dating from 1914. Open daily from 8am. CW9 5AB
NORTHWICH SEAFARER - Watling Street. Tel: 01606 43169. Fish & chip restaurant & takeaway. CW9 5AF

Shopping
Excellent retail market Tue, Fri & Sat. Carbon footprint-free fruit and veg from First Choice Fruit on Leicester Street. Fine butchers called Webb & Son (est 1929) on Witton Street whose motto is 'maintain thine honour and extend thy fame', and whose pork pies are a pretty much permanent fixture in Pearson's 'Desert Island' list of pies. Sainsbury's supermarket on Venables Road. Branch of Waitrose alongside Northwich Quay. Bratts department store in the High Street is worthy of note, and can trace its origins back to the Victorian era, and has connections (on the distaff side) with Pimblotts. An Asda supermarket is promised at Baron's Quay.

Things to Do
TOURIST INFORMATION - The Arcade, Watling Street. Tel: 01606 288815. CW9 5AS
WEAVER HALL MUSEUM - London Road. Tel: 01606 271640. History and heritage of mid-Cheshire housed in a former workhouse. Previously known as the Salt Museum, the emphasis has changed in deference to the multi-million pound development of the Lion Salt Works at Marston - see page 8. CW9 8AB

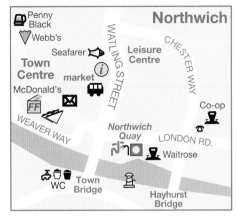

Connections
BUSES - useful links with Trent & Mersey at Barnton, Anderton etc; also to/from Winsford and Acton Bridge for walks along the Weaver. Tel: 0871 200 2233.
TRAINS - local services to/from Chester, Stockport & Manchester along the scenic mid-Cheshire line from station approx one mile east of town centre. Take the train to Delamere and walk in the woods. Tel: 08457 484950.
TAXIS - JJ's. Tel: 01606 76262.

Winsford
Map 45

Surprisingly large, and not especially likeable, Winsford's modern centre lies to the west of the river, a turgid hike from the visitor moorings at Winsford Bridges. On the east bank of the river a Morrisons supermarket is fairly accessible, as is the Wharton Park, a Crown Carvery - Tel: 01606 558729 CW7 3DB. There are two pubs, a bar and a pizza take-away adjacent to Winsford Bridges. Imagine how popular the Weaver might be if there was a *Nantwich* at its southern extremity.

Acton Bridge
Map 46

Scattered community on hillside overlooking the Trent & Mersey Canal and the River Weaver. Popular with boaters on both waterways on account of the close proximity of a number of good pubs and eating places. Lots of nice local walks to be had, or longer explorations along the Weaver Way.

Eating & Drinking
DAVENPORT'S FARM SHOP - Warrington Road. (Bridge 209). Tel: 01606 853241. Cafe serving breakfasts (10am-11.30am), lunches (11.30am-3pm), and afternoon teas (1pm-3pm). Closed Tuesdays. CW8 4QU
HAZEL PEAR - adjacent Acton Bridge railway station. Tel: 01606 853195. Charming and comfortably refurbished inn whose name recalls fruit being grown commercially in the district. Food. CW8 3RA
HOLLY BUSH - Warrington Road. Tel: 01606 853196. 16th Century thatched pub on A49 beyond Trent & Mersey Canal. Food and accommodation. CW8 4QY.
LEIGH ARMS - Warrington Road. Tel: 01606 853327. Comfortable Robinson's outpost overlooking Acton Swing Bridge. Intriguing painted windows featuring local scenes, not least the Weaver Navigation. CW8 4QT
THE MAYPOLE - Hill Top Road. Tel: 01606 853114. Comfortable country pub in village centre. CW8 3RA
THE RIVERSIDE - Warrington Road. Tel: 01606 852310. Marston's 'Two for One' restaurant with customer moorings and waterside patio. CW8 3QD

Shopping
DAVENPORT'S FARM SHOP - Tel: 01606 853241. Award-winning farm shop offering food and drink from upwards of fifty regionally based suppliers. Nice line in bottled beer. CW8 4QU *Not open Tuesdays.*

Connections
BUSES - services to/from Northwich and Warrington. Tel: 0871 200 2233.

TRAINS - Acton Bridge railway station can be a useful staging point for towpath walkers, but be warned that the timetable is comparatively sparse. Tel: 08457 484950

Up on the busy waters of the Trent & Mersey you can count the cabin tops of passing boats. Down here on the Weaver you sense that you've escaped a considerable distance from Gray and Hardy's 'madding crowd'. Acton Swing Bridge and Dutton Lock thus provoke welcome interludes of interest. Tall Lombardy poplar trees are a recurring feature of the riverbank, delineating its progress along the valley's pasturelands.

The river splits into two channels at Acton Bridge. The northernmost is the main, the southern having been adopted for linear moorings by the local cruising club. Impressively muscular, Acton Swing Bridge spans both channels, pivoting on a central pontoon. It dates from 1933: evidence of an earlier bridge lies adjacent, one arch still spanning the smaller, boat-filled channel.

Dutton Lock demands a degree of concentration, but compensates with the opportunity to pass the time of day with the resident lock-keeper. Visually it is typical of the river's modernised locks, replete with redundant semaphore signals and dual chambers. The partially capsized wreck of the MV *Chica* has been a feature of Dutton for a number of years. Oddly enough it began its chequered career as a Norwegian sailing vessel at the end of the 19th Century.

Downstream the old towpath is carried across the original navigation channel upon an elegant timber side-bridge dated 1919. But, as bridges go, it is Joseph Locke's Dutton (or Weaver) Viaduct, built in 1837 for the Grand Junction Railway, that steals the scene, its sandstone arches reflecting handsomely in the river. The lock at Pickerings was eliminated at the end of the Second World War and the residents of the two houses on the north bank have to cross the river - with their groceries and chattels - by boat. West of here the Weaver goes all shy and retiring, becoming the haunt of otters and cormorants, and negotiating a series of luxuriantly wooded reaches which remind one forcibly of the navigable reaches of Devon's River Dart.

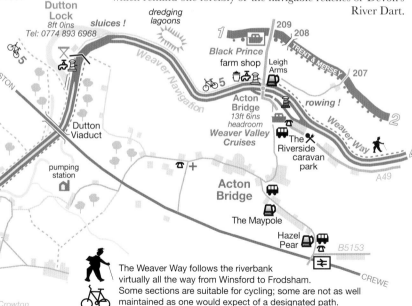

Dutton Lock
8ft 0ins
Tel: 0774 893 6968

sluices !

dredging lagoons

PRESTON

1

209 208

207

2

Black Prince farm shop

Leigh Arms

Weaver Navigation

Dutton Viaduct

Acton Bridge
13ft 6ins headroom

rowing !

Weaver Way

44

A49

site of Pickerings Lock

Weaver Valley Cruises

The Riverside caravan park

Weaver Way

pumping station

Acton Bridge

Crewood Hall

The Maypole

47

N

Hazel Pear

B5153

"Devil's Garden"

CREWE

by-road to Crowton & Cooksongreen

The Weaver Way follows the riverbank virtually all the way from Winsford to Frodsham. Some sections are suitable for cycling; some are not as well maintained as one would expect of a designated path.

WAS it something Mr Nicholson said? Do boaters still think the lower reaches of the Weaver are busily commercial? On a warm August weekday we saw only two boats on the move. True, the river begins to shed its rural charm as it approaches the outskirts of Frodsham, and boaters with a highly-tuned aesthetic scale of values may prefer to proceed no further than the site of Sutton Lock, but that's no reason for not exploring downstream of Dutton. Go on, indulge your inner explorer!

Frodsham Cut is protected by a boom, reedy and unnavigable. In the first print run of this edition we advocated walking along the cut to see if *Panary* (a 1937 built barge) or the ex 'Brunner' *James Jackson Grundy* (built by Yarwoods in 1947) were berthed at Frodsham Quay with cargoes of grain from Seaforth. But these days they are rumoured to discharge more often at Runcorn Docks.

Three bridges span the navigation as it pursues an artificial course to the east of Frodsham. One is a typical Weaver swing bridge, one a lofty railway bridge, and one a modern motorway structure. Just past the premises of Runcorn Rowing Club are Rock Savage visitor moorings, the lowest downstream on the Weaver. The vast Ineos chemical plants dominate the last mile of the Weaver Navigation.

Weston Marsh Lock leads down into the Manchester Ship Canal. Without special

arrangement, craft licensed with the Canal & River Trust cannot proceed any further unless they opt to explore the short Weston Canal leading to Weston Point Docks. Neither can the docks (just beyond the left hand edge of the accompanying map) be accessed, but there is room for doughty inland waterway navigators to turn their craft. Moribund for a number of years, this facility is earmarked for redevelopment as the intermodal Port of Weston. To discuss access for suitably seaworthy and properly insured inland vessels to the MSC at either Weston Marsh Lock or the Port of Weston telephone 0151 327 1461.

Regrettably, for those who like to cruise in circles, the Runcorn & Weston Canal no longer links with the Bridgewater Canal at Runcorn. Perhaps the last authenticated journey along this missing link was John Seymour's *Voyage Into England* in the mid Sixties. Though already officially abandoned, he managed to effect a passage, much to the consternation of the authorities who were left with no option other than to run vast quantities of water down from the Bridgewater to facilitate recovery of the Seymours' boat from the closed canal. Nowadays we must return the way we came, though given the Weaver's inherent beauty, that is no great burden.

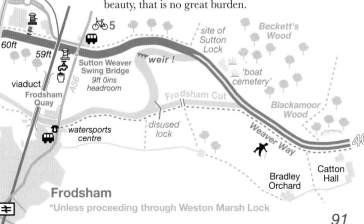

Runcorn Rowing Club **12**

rowing !

WEAVER NAVIGATION

site of swing bridge

60ft

59ft

viaduct

Frodsham Quay

Sutton Weaver Swing Bridge
9ft 0ins headroom

5

site of Sutton Lock

weir !

Beckett's Wood

'boat cemetery'

Frodsham Cut

Weaver Way

Blackamoor Wood

46

Ineos Fluor

Ineos Chlor

WESTON CANAL

Weston Marsh Lock

River Weaver

M'cstr Ship Canal

Point

To Eastham

Helsby Hill

5

M56

watersports centre

disused lock

Bradley Orchard

Catton Hall

Frodsham Marsh

N

Frodsham

*Unless proceeding through Weston Marsh Lock

This Guide

Pearson's Canal Companions are a long established, independently produced series of guide books devoted to the inland waterways and designed to appeal equally to boaters, walkers, cyclists and other, less readily pigeon-holed members of society. Considerable pride is taken to make these guides as up to date, accurate, entertaining and inspirational as possible. A good guide book should fulfil three functions: make you want to go; interpret the lie of the land when you're there; and provide a lasting souvenir of your journeys.

The Maps

There are forty-seven numbered maps whose layout is shown by the Route Planner inside the front cover. Maps 1 to 22 cover the Trent & Mersey Canal in its entirety from Preston Brook to Derwentmouth (Sawley); Maps 13 and 23 to 27 cover the northern half of the Staffordshire & Worcestershire Canal; and Maps 27 to 40 cover the Shropshire Union from Autherley via Barbridge to Middlewich. The Caldon Canal, a branch of the Trent & Mersey, appears on Maps 8 and 41 to 43. The Weaver Navigation is featured on Maps 44 to 47. Boaters navigating the Four Counties Ring should use Maps 4 to 13, and 23 to 40.

The maps - measured imperially like the waterways they depict, and not being slavishly north-facing - are easily read in either direction. Users will thus find most itineraries progressing smoothly and logically from left to right or vice versa. Figures quoted at the top of each map refer to distance per map, locks per map and average cruising time. An alternative indication of timings from centre to centre can be found on the Route Planner. Obviously, cruising times vary with the nature of your boat and the number of crew at your disposal, so quoted times should be taken only as an estimate. Neither do times quoted take into account any delays which might occur at lock flights in high season. Walking and cycling times will depend

INFORMATION

very much on the state of individual sections of towpath and the stamina of those concerned.

The Text

Each map is accompanied by a route commentary placing the waterway in its historic, social and topographical context. As close to each map as is feasible, gazetteer-like entries are given for places passed through, listing, where appropriate, facilities of significance to users of this guide. Every effort is made to ensure these details are as up to date as possible, but - especially where pubs/restaurants are concerned - we suggest you telephone ahead if relying upon an entry to provide you with a meal at any given time.

Walking

The simplest way to go canal exploring is on foot along the towpaths originally provided so that horses could 'tow' boats. Walking costs little more than the price of shoe leather and you are free to concentrate on the passing scene; something that boaters, with the responsibilities of navigation thrust upon them, are not always at liberty to do. The maps set out to give some idea of the quality of the towpath on any given section of canal. More of an art than a science to be sure, but at least it reflects our personal experiences, and whilst it does vary from area to area, none of it should prove problematical for anyone inured to the vicissitudes of country walking. We recommend the use of public transport to facilitate 'one-way' itineraries but stress the advisability of checking up to date details on the telephone numbers quoted, or on the websites of National Rail Enquiries or Traveline for trains and buses respectively.

Cycling

Bicycling along towpaths is an increasingly popular pastime, though one not always equally popular with other waterway users such as boaters, anglers and pedestrians. It is important to remember that you are sharing the towpath with other people out for their own form of enjoyment, and to treat them with the respect and politeness they deserve. A bell is a useful form of diplomacy; failing that, a stentorian cough.

Happily, with the inception of the Canal & River Trust in 2012, it became no longer necessary for cyclists to acquire a permit to use the towpath.

Boating

Boating on inland waterways is an established, though relatively small, facet of the UK tourist industry. It is also, increasingly, a chosen lifestyle. There are approximately 30,000 privately owned boats registered on the canals, but in addition to these, numerous firms offer boats for hire. These range from small operators with half a dozen boats to sizeable fleets run by companies with several bases.

Most hire craft have all the creature comforts you are likely to expect. In the excitement of planning a boating holiday you may give scant thought to the contents of your hire boat, but at the end of a hard day's boating such matters take on more significance, and a well equipped, comfortable boat, large enough to accommodate your crew with something to spare, can make the difference between a good holiday and one which will be shudderingly remembered for the wrong reasons.

Traditionally, hire boats are booked out by the week or fortnight, though many firms now offer more flexible short breaks or extended weeks. All reputable hire firms give newcomers tuition in boat handling and lock working, and first-timers soon find themselves adapting to the pace of things 'on the cut'.

Navigational Advice

Newcomers, hiring a boat on the inland waterways for the first time, have every right to expect sympathetic and thorough tuition from the company providing their boat. Boat-owners are, by definition, likely to be already adept at navigating. The following, however, may prove useful points of reference.

Locks are part of the charm of canal cruising, but they are potentially dangerous environments for children, pets and careless adults. Use of them should be methodical and unhurried, whilst special care should be exercised in rain, frost and snow when slippery hazards abound. The majority of locks featured in this guide are of the narrow variety, but on the Trent & Mersey *east* of Burton-on-Trent they are widebeam and can fit two narrowboats side by side. On the Weaver they are very large and manned and we would urge newcomers to the river to seek advice from the keepers on duty until they become familiar with procedures.

A few locks in areas prone to vandalism are fitted with 'Water Conservation Keys' which can be obtained from chandleries and CART offices. Finally, it behoves us all to be on our best behaviour at locks. Remember to exercise a little 'give and take'. The use of foul mouths or fists to decide precedence at locks is one canal tradition not worthy of preservation.

Mooring on the canals featured in this guide is per usual practice - ie on the towpath side, away from sharp bends, bridge-holes and narrows. A 'yellow' bollard symbol represents visitor mooring sites; either as designated officially or, in some cases, as recommended by our personal experience. Of course, one of the great joys of canal boating has always been the ability to moor wherever (sensibly) you like. In recent years, however, it has become obvious, particularly in urban areas, that there are an increasing number of undesirable locations where mooring is not to be recommended for fear of vandalism, theft or abuse. It would be nice if local authorities would see their way to providing pleasant, secure, overnight facilities for passing boaters who, after all, bring the commerce of tourism in their wake. Few boaters would object to making a small payment in such circumstances, as is the custom on a number of river navigations.

Turning points on the canals are known as 'winding holes'; pronounced as the thing which blows because in the old days the wind was expected to do much of the work rather than the boatman. Winding holes capable of taking a full length boat of around seventy foot length are marked where appropriate on the maps. Winding holes capable of turning shorter craft are marked with the approximate length. It is of course also possible to turn boats at junctions and at most boatyards, though in the case of the latter it is considered polite to request permission before doing so.

Tunnels occur at a number of points on the canals and are great fun to negotiate, but to be on the safe side pets and young children should be kept 'indoors'. Don't forget to put your headlight on as you enter and to turn it off when you emerge at the other end. Many tunnels 'leak', so remove your Canal Companion to a place of safety!

Boating facilities are provided at regular intervals along the inland waterways, and range from a simple water tap or refuse disposal skip, to the provision of sewage disposal, showers and laundry. Such vital features are also obtainable at boatyards and marinas along with repairs and servicing. An alphabetical list of boatyards appears on pages 94-5.

Closures (or 'stoppages' in canal parlance) traditionally occur on the inland waterways between November and April, during which time most of the heavy maintenance work is undertaken. Occasionally, however, an emergency stoppage, or perhaps water restriction, may be imposed at short notice, closing part of the route you intend to use. Up to date details are available on *www.waterscape.com* or from hire bases.

Harecastle Tunnel - a timetable of entry periods operates through the 'single-lane' tunnel at Harecastle on Map 7. In the interest of safety the tunnel is only open when manned by the tunnel-keepers who have offices adjacent to the north and south portals of the tunnel. operating times are as follows:
WINTER HOURS - November to mid-March. The tunnel is only open by appointment Mon-Sat. Telephone 0303 040 4040 giving at least 48 hours notice.
NORMAL HOURS - mid-March to mid-May and mid-September to end of October. The tunnel is open for passage between 8am and 5pm. *To be guaranteed a passage craft must arrive by 3pm.*
SUMMER HOURS - mid-May to mid-September. As above but open until 6pm. *For last guaranteed passage arrive by 4pm.*

Weaver Navigation - boaters wishing to use Anderton Lift to reach the Weaver from the Trent & Mersey may do so free of charge on the day but it is advisable to pre-book (for which, paradoxically, there is a fee) by telephoning the Canal & River Trust on 01606 786777. Note also that the locks on the Weaver are subject to restricted opening times, further details being available from the above contact. In case of difficulty we append the lock-keeper's mobile number on the map at each lock.
continued overleaf:

continued from page 93:

Useful Contacts
Canal & River Trust
The Canal & River Trust controls the bulk of the inland waterways network. Their Head Office is located at:
First Floor North, Station House
500 Elder Gate, Milton Keynes
MK9 1BB
Tel: 0303 040 4040
www.canalrivertrust.org.uk

Societies
The Inland Waterways Association was founded in 1946 to campaign for the retention of the canal system. Many routes now open to pleasure boaters may not have been so but for this organisation. Membership details, together with details of the IWA's regional branches, may be obtained from: Inland Waterways Association, Island House, Moor Road, Chesham HP5 1WA. Tel: 01494 783453. www.waterways.org.uk A number of the canals featured in this guide are also supported by individual societies.
Derby & Sandiacre Canal Society
Lichfield & Hatherton Canals Restoration Trust
River Weaver Navigation Society
Shropshire Union Canal Society
Staffordshire & Worcestershire Canal Society
Trent & Mersey Canal Society

Acknowledgements
Grateful thanks on the occasion of this 30th Anniversary edition to everyone involved down the years. Specific thanks for this publication, however, are due: Meg Gregory for the sign-written cover artwork; to Karen Tanguy who facilitated the author's research trips and generally ensured the book's smooth passage to the printers; and to those selfsame printers, Hawksworth of Uttoxeter, and all their staff.

BOATING DIRECTORY

Boat Hire

ABC BOAT HIRE - Anderton, Trent & Mersey Canal, Map 2, and Gailey, Staffs & Worcs Canal Map 25, PO Box 232, Worcester WR1 2SD Tel: 0330 333 0590. www.abcboathire.com

ANDERSEN BOATS - Middlewich, Trent & Mersey, Map 4. Wych House Lane, Middlewich, Cheshire CW10 9BQ Tel: 01606 833668. www.andersenboats.com

ANGLO WELSH - Great Haywood, Trent & Mersey Canal, Map 13; Bunbury Wharf, Shropshire Union Canal, Map 38. 2 The Hide Market, West Street, Bristol BS2 0BH Tel: 0117 304 1122. www.anglowelsh.co.uk

AQUA NARROWBOATS - Mercia Marina, Trent & Mersey Canal, Map 20. Findern Lane, Willington, Derbyshire DE65 6DW Tel: 01283 701041. www.aquanarrowboats.co.uk

AVANTE CLASSIC - Mercia Marina, Trent & Mersey Canal, Map 20. Findern Lane, Willington. Derbyshire DE65 6DW Tel: 01926 844249. www.boatingholidayrentals.co.uk

BLACK PRINCE HOLIDAYS - Bartington Wharf, Trent & Mersey, Map 1, and Etruria, Trent & Mersey, Map 8. Stoke Prior, Bromsgrove, Worcestershire B60 4LA Tel: 01527 575115. www.black-prince.com

CANAL CRUISING - Stone, Trent & Mersey Canal, Map 10. The Wharf, Crown Street, Stone, Staffordshire ST15 8QN Tel: 01785 813982. www.canalcruising.co.uk

CHESHIRE CAT - Audlem, Shropshire Union, Map 35. Lock House, Chester Road, Hurleston CW5 6BU Tel: 0786 779 0195. www.cheshirecatnarrowboats.co.uk

CLAYMOORE NARROWBOATS - Preston Brook, Bridgewater Canal, Map 1. The Wharf, Preston Brook, Warrington WA4 4BA Tel: 01928 717273. www.claymoore.co.uk

COUNTRYWIDE CRUISERS - Brewood, Shropshire Union Canal, Map 28. The Wharf, Brewood, Staffordshire ST19 9BG Tel: 01902 850166. www.countrywide-cruisers.com

HIRE A CANAL BOAT - Sawley Marina, River Trent, Map 22. Sawley Marina, Long Eaton, Nottinghamshire NG10 3AE Tel: 01707 655649. www.hireacanalboat.co.uk

MARINE CRUISES - Kings Bromley Wharf, Trent & Mersey Canal, Map 15. WS13 8HT Tel: 01244 373911. www.marinecruises.co.uk

MIDDLEWICH NARROWBOATS - Middlewich, Trent & Mersey Canal, Map 4. Canal Terrace, Middlewich, Cheshire CW10 9BD Tel: 01606 832460. www.middlewichnarrowboats.co.uk

MIDWAY BOATS - Barbridge Marina, Shropshire Union Canal, Map 38. CW5 6BE Tel: 01270 528482. www.midwayboats.co.uk Day Hire Only

NANTWICH CANAL CENTRE - Nantwich, Shropshire Union Canal, Map 37. CW5 8LB Tel: 01270 625122. www.nantwichcc.co.uk Day Hire Only

NAPTON NARROWBOATS - Autherley, Shropshire Union Canal, Map 27. Autherley Junction, Oxley Moor Road, Wolverhampton WV9 5HW Tel: 01902 789942. www.napton-marina.co.uk

NORBURY WHARF - Norbury, Shropshire Union Canal, Map 31. The Wharf, Norbury Junction, Staffordshire ST20 0PN Tel: 01785 284292. www.norburyhire.co.uk

VENETIAN - Venetian Marina, Middlewich Arm, Map 39. Poole, Nantwich, Cheshire CW5 6DD. Tel: 01270 528122. www.venetianhireboats.co.uk

Boatyards

ANDERTON MARINA - Anderton, Trent & Mersey Canal, Map 2. Tel: 01606 79642. CW9 6AJ

ANGLO-WELSH - Great Haywood, Trent & Mersey Canal, Map 13. Tel: 01889 881711. ST18 0RJ; Bunbury, Shropshire Union Canal, Map 38. Tel: 01829 260957. CW6 9QB

AQUEDUCT MARINA - Church Minshull, Shropshire Union, Middlewich Branch, Map 39. Tel: 01270 525041. CW5 6DX

BARNTON WHARF - Barnton, Trent & Mersey Canal, Map 2. Tel: 01606 783320. CW8 4EP

BARTON MARINA - Barton-under-Needwood, Trent & Mersey, Map 17. Tel: 01283 711666. DE13 8DZ

BLACK PRINCE (BARTINGTON) - Bartington, Trent & Mersey, Map 1. Tel: 01606 852945. CW8 4QU

BLACK PRINCE (STOKE) - Etruria, Trent & Mersey Canal, Map 8. Tel: 01782 201981. ST1 5PA

CANAL CRUISING - Stone, Trent & Mersey Canal, Map 10. Tel: 01785 813982. ST15 8QN

CHAPEL FARM MARINA - Shardlow, Trent & Mersey Canal, Map 22. Tel: 01332 799561. DE72 2HF

DOLPHIN BOATS - Stoke-on-Trent, Trent & Mersey Canal, Map 8. Tel: 01782 849390. ST4 4HW

ELTON MOSS BOAT BUILDERS - Sandbach, Trent & Mersey, Map 5. Tel: 01270 760770. CW11 3PW

GREAT HAYWOOD MARINA - Great Haywood, Trent & Mersey Canal, Map 12. Tel: 01889 883713. ST18 0RQ

JD BOAT SERVICES - Gailey, Staffs & Worcs Canal, Map 25. Tel: 01902 791811. ST19 5PR

JD NARROWBOATS - Shardlow, Trent & Mersey Canal, Map 22. Tel: 01332 792271. DE72 2GJ

KINGS BROMLEY MARINA - Kings Bromley, Trent & Mersey Canal, Map 15. Tel: 01543 417209. WS13 8HT

KINGS LOCK CHANDLERY - Middlewich, Trent & Mersey Canal, Map 4. Tel: 01606 737564. CW10 0JJ

MARINE SERVICES FRADLEY - Fradley, Trent & Mersey Canal, Map 16. Tel: 01283 790332. DE13 7DN

MERCIA MARINA - Willington, Trent & Mersey Canal, Map 19. Tel: 01283 703332. DE65 6DW

MIDDLEWICH N'BOATS - Middlewich, Trent & Mersey, Map 4. Tel: 01606 832460. CW10 9BD

MIDLAND CANAL CENTRE - Stenson, Trent & Mersey Canal, Map 20. Tel: 01283 701933. DE73 7HL

MIDWAY BOATS - Barbridge, Shropshire Union Canal, Map 43. Tel: 01270 528682. CW5 6BE

NANTWICH CANAL CENTRE - Nantwich, Shropshire Union, Map 37. Tel: 01270 625122. CW5 8LB

NORBURY WHARF - Norbury Junction, Shropshire Union, Map 31. Tel: 01785 284292. ST20 0PN

NORTHWICH QUAY - Northwich, Weaver Navigation, Map 44. Tel: 01606 354405. CW9 5JJ

ORCHARD MARINA - Higher Shurlach, Trent & Mersey Canal, Map 3. Tel: 01606 42082. CW9 7RG

ORWELLS BOATYARD - Market Drayton, Shropshire Union, Map 34. Tel: 01630 652472. TF9 4BH

OTHERTON BOAT HAVEN - Penkridge, Staffs & Worcs Canal, Map 29. Tel: 01785 712515. ST19 5NX

OVERWATER MARINA - Audlem, Shropshire Union Canal, Map 35. Tel: 01270 812677. CW5 8AY

SAWLEY MARINA - Sawley, Trent Navigation, Map 22. Tel: 0115 907 7400. NG10 3AE

SHARDLOW MARINA - Shardlow, Trent Navigation, Map 22. Tel: 01332 792832. DE72 2GL

SHOBNALL MARINA - Burton-on-Trent, Trent & Mersey Canal, Map 18. Tel: 01283 542718. DE14 2AU

STOKE-ON-TRENT BOATBUILDING - Longport, Trent & Mersey Canal, Map 7. Tel: 01782 813831. ST6 4NB

STONE BOAT BUILDING - Stone, Trent & Mersey Canal, Map 10. Tel: 01785 812688. ST15 8JZ

TALBOT WHARF - Market Drayton, Shropshire Union Canal, Map 34. Tel: 01630 652641. TF9 1HN

TEDDESLEY BOAT CO - Penkridge, Staffs & Worcs Canal, Map 24. Tel: 01785 714692. ST19 5RH

UPLANDS BASIN MARINA - Anderton, Trent & Mersey Canal, Map 2. Tel: 01606 782986. CW9 6AJ

VENETIAN MARINA - Cholmondeston, Shropshire Union Canal, Map 44. Tel: 01270 528251. CW5 6DA

WINCHAM WHARF CANAL CENTRE - Wincham, Trent & Mersey Canal, Map 3. Tel: 01606 44672 CW9 7NT

Nine More Reasons for Exploring the Canals with Pearsons

9th edition - ISBN 978 0 9562777 3 2

10th edition - ISBN 978 0 9562777 8 7

9th edition - ISBN 978 0 9562777 7 0

1st edition - ISBN 978 0 9928492 1

7th edition - ISBN 978 0 9562777 5 6

8th edition - ISBN 978 0 9562777 2 5

8th edition - ISBN 978 0 9562777 9 4

1st edition - ISBN 978 0 9928492 0 7

3rd edition - ISBN 978 0 9562777 6 3

Pearson's Canal Companions are published by Wayzgoose. They are widely available from hire bases, boatyards, canal shops, good bookshops, via Amazon and other internet outlets.